Lone Fir: The Cemetery

LONE FIR
THE CEMETERY

A GUIDE & HISTORY

JOHAN MATHIESEN

DEADMANTALKING
PORTLAND, OREGON

DeadManTalking
3044 SE 9th Avenue
Portland, OR 97202

Book set in 11 pt. Palantino type face; heads in Papyrus.

All photographs by the author.

A portion of the proceeds from this book go to support the Lone Fir Foundation.

ISBN-13: 978-0615644943

To J.B. Stephens
We'll be with you, bye-and-bye.

TABLE OF CONTENTS

Thanks, Everyone

IF IT HADN'T BEEN FOR J. B. STEPHENS, there never would have been a Lone Fir and no need for this guide, so a tip of the toque to "Pappy." And the Good Lord only knows what would have happened to the place if plans to sell it hadn't fallen through, so hats off to Metro for biting the bullet and deciding to be pro-active in caring for its fourteen cemeteries. Likewise, thanks to Rachel Fox who has taken on her duties full-bore ahead and is crafting a future for the Metro cemeteries. Thanks, of course, to the Friends of Lone Fir for continually fighting on her behalf and for taking her to their bosom. She would not have the recognition she has were it not for the Friends. But most of all, thanks to Portland for being Portland. We know we're darn lucky to be here.

As always, my heart goes to my wife. In the not too distant future, we'll join J. B. and Elizabeth for as long as eternity lasts around here. We were among the last to secure ground in the venerable graveyard. Luck, it seems, will follow me to the grave.

Come visit.

JAMES B. STEPHENS,
EAST PORTLAND, OR.

Nature's Immutable Laws

Here we lie by consent, after 57 years 2 months and 2 days
sojourning through life awaiting nature's immutable laws
to return us back to the elements of the universe, of which
we were first composed.
    Epitaph: James (1806-1889) & Elizabeth (1805-1887)
                                        Stephens

ROUGHLY THIRTY ACRES IN A RECTANGLE twice as long as wide,
Lone Fir Cemetery is the finest Portland arboretum east
of the Willamette River. From within, it is largely flat with
gentle undulations and a slight rise towards the northwest
corner. The lone fir has been joined by a diverse forest of
now mature trees and a heritage rose garden. Lovers stroll
the arbored lanes, joggers patrol the roads, mothers and fa-
thers push baby carriages around the loop. Musicians play,
students read, children run from stone to stone exclaiming,
"Look at this!"

The Russians tend their gardens, coaxing splashes of color
onto the shade-dappled lawn. Old people shuffle through
the granite forest looking for family or history or both. Cars
slowly drive through. Bikes use it as a thoroughfare. Friends
stop by and have lunch. It's a cemetery, yes, but it's every bit
as much a park stuffed with a century-and-a-half's worth
of art and stories. In the heart of Portland's vibrant Eastside, Lone Fir is precisely what cemeteries were originally
designed to be: graceful, natural landscapes adorned with
edifying monuments.

It wasn't always that way. In fact, when Portland was first given the opportunity in 1866 to buy the cemetery from its owner, Colburn Barrell, they turned him down flat. Too far from town, they said. A newspaper columnist of the era expressed his concerns in a column entitled "Letter From Oregon"[1]:

Properly speaking the burial of the dead and the custody of the place of their sepulture belongs to the churches. Another serious objection to this municipal cemetery is that it involves to a certain extent the modern tendency to agrarianism—by turning private wants and responsibilities into public ones and imposing the cost and duty of meeting them upon the public purse. To the extent that this is practiced and allowed it puts the loafer and the spendthrift upon the level with the industrious and economical, at the expense of the latter.

Fortunately, a trio of citizens, Levi Anderson, Robert Pittock, and Byron Cardwell, disagreed and purchased the property from Barrell for $5,100.[2] Barrell made a tidy profit on the sale, which was more than he was accustomed to doing. He ended out evicted from his home and died penniless; an ignominious fate for the grandson of Joseph Barrell, one of the three Boston sponsors of Captain Gray's 1792 voyage which discovered, for America, the mouth of the Columbia.[3]

Colburn's role in Lone Fir is unmistakable and well documented. It was he who legally organized the first cemetery on the Eastside and he functioned as its first sexton and gravedigger. His original price was $20 a lot and he threw in opening the grave. Beyond that, the early history of Lone Fir is somewhat confused.

What's not confused is the original name of the cemetery, Mt. Crawford. Approached from the entrances on the east and south sides, the slight rise of the land towards the northwest corner is not particularly noticeable unless you're in that part of the cemetery, but if you were to walk along 20th Ave. to the west, you'd see there's a fair lift between the street and the graveyard. Most of the hill along 20th Ave. has been leveled for the building of homes and businesses; but that's the hill that inspired calling it "mount." "Crawford" was in reference to Colburn's best friend, Crawford Dobbins, who was killed in 1854 in a boiler accident aboard the steamer Gazelle at Oregon Falls (known as Canemah, at the time).[4] Dobbins is often, erroneously, credited with being the first burial in Lone Fir (even though a quantity of other passengers from the steamer were buried along with Dobbins; and, furthermore, Dobbins was originally buried in a "north Portland cemetery, but after lying about a year [was] removed across the river"[5]).

That honor would go to Emmor Stephens, who died in 1846. There's no question that Emmor and his son and daughter-in-law, the source of the opening quote, are buried in the northwest corner of Lone Fir, the original set-aside; and there's no argument that Emmor died in 1846. There's not much question as to where he was originally buried.

Despite other histories to the contrary, it's doubtful that Barrell bought any land from Stephens. If he did, no one has found traces of it. Stephens sold land to the likes of Ainsworth, Buckman, and Ladd, but not, apparently, Barrell. If Barrell did buy land from Stephens, it wasn't for Lone Fir, as the land which Lone Fir occupies is on Seldon Murray's original Donation Land Claim. Murray sold ten acres of it to Barrell in 1855 for the "consideration of the sum of One hundred Dollars [reputedly in gold coin]... for Cemetary [sic] purposes forever."[6] According to documents in the Oregon Historical Society, Barrell had talked to Murray about setting aside ten acres for a cemetery as early as 1852; but by

that time it was already a cemetery. It's worth noting that the restrictive clause confining the use of the ten-acres to a cemetery was inserted by Murray, not Barrell. Murray had made his promise to Stephens.

Once Barrell had taken over the cemetery, he rapidly went about expanding into the surrounding neighborhood. In May of 1856 an unpaginated abstract of deeds in the OHS library for 1855 through 1858 records a sale between Barrell and one Geo. Bagby of $400 for forty acres:

> Commencing on the northern line of S. Murray claim
> (which is also his base line) at the distance of 40 rods from
> from the northwest corner of sd. [said] claim, and at the
> N. E. corner of Crawford Cemetery, thence south along sd.
> cemetery line and east line of A. Campbell's land 120 rods
> thence E. 50 rods thence [north] 120 rods to the base line,
> thence W. 50 rods to the place of beginning. Containing 40
> acres of ld [land].[7]

This plot would have contained the entire rest of the cemetery and then some, save for a strip adjoining the original ten acres on the south, Blocks 13 and 14, including the Chinese cemetery. Bagby had bought the forty acres from Murray[8] the previous October, shortly after Barrell bought the cemetery. In the same year, the land including Blocks 13 and 14 was purchased by Barrell from George and Mary Robbins.

In that transaction Barrell bought twenty acres for $400. In all, he controlled seventy acres out of which he carved the thirty-acre cemetery. There are several accounts of Barrell adding acreage to the cemetery in thirteen and seven-acre installments, but those additions had to come from his existing land, most of which he later sold to Ladd.[9]

How Emmor Stephens got buried on Murray's claim is open to speculation. He could have been moved there (like Dobbins was), but there's no evidence for that. He could have been buried there by mistake, although Seldon Murray knew where there was "a stake signifying the corner of said Murray claim on the North West and corner of the Stephens claim on the North East."[10] Emmor was buried west of that stake, some 300 feet into Murray property on the penultimate shelf of the hill looking west towards the river and the new town of Portland. Stephens may have been a ferry operator,[11] but he made his fortune in land speculation. He was rapidly cutting up and selling off his property, and it's hard to imagine he wouldn't have known where that stake was, too. Or that Murray wouldn't have noticed the grave.

I think it happened this way.

James B. Stephens and Seldon Murray split the core of east side Portland between them. Their Donation Land Claims were side-by-each and ran between Cesar Chavez Blvd. (old 39th Ave.) and the river. The north-south street, 20th

Ave., divided their properties and Stephens held everything west from there to the river, and Murray held everything east towards Cesar Chavez. The dividing line, 20th Ave., runs along the eastern border of Ladd's Addition. People who frequently travel 20th Ave. know that at the northern and southern ends of 20th Ave. where it borders Ladd's, it kinks slightly westward making for odd intersections. The imaginary line separating the land claims didn't make that little kink but rather continued on straight, which means it ran parallel to 20th but slightly east of it. For the most part, the offset of that line doesn't have a huge impact on the cityscape, aside from the kinking street, except for the Lone Fir blocks. The cemetery does extend westward to precisely where the claim division line runs, which leaves a strip of property between the cemetery and 20th Ave. occupied by businesses and residences rather than by the cemetery, as one would expect.

Stephens, having the riverside claim, had the best of the bargain in developing early Portland as she pushed east over the Willamette, and he easily had enough money to erect the impressive monument to himself and his wife in Lone Fir. When J. B.'s father, Emmor died in 1846, J. B. wanted to bury him on the highest point on his property from which he could survey everything he owned; and that point would

be the extreme northeast corner of his property, right where that little strip of land along 20th Ave butted up against Murray's land. No problem with that, except that Stephens only held title to the west-facing skirt of the hill, the crest belonged to Murray. It would be unseemly to bury Dad in the lowly strip of land where there was no commanding view. For that, one needed the summit.

That's when, I believe, Stephens had a conversation with Murray that is attributed to being with Colburn Barrell. I think Stephens asked Murray if he could bury his father on the crest of the hill and could the land be permanently dedicated as a cemetery? I think Murray agreed and that's how Emmor came to be buried on Murray property, and that agreement was written into the deed that Murray sold Barrell. Effectively, that was the beginning of Lone Fir, a half-dozen years before Colburn Barrell entered the discussion. Colburn Barrell one way or another heard of the promise and by 1852 was talking with Murray about future plans for the cemetery. What pushed the conversation out of the speculative and into the concrete was the aforementioned death of Colburn's best friend, Crawford Dobbins. Dobbins (along with other unfortunates) was the second burial and the eponym for the first iteration of the cemetery: Mt. Crawford Cemetery. He was buried there in 1855 the year Seldon Murray signed over the first ten acres of Lone Fir.

Over the Barrells

When Barrell sold the cemetery, its name changed, following the suggestion of Mrs. Barrell, Aurelia, who proposed, to unanimous acclaim, "Lone Fir" in honor of the single tree

still standing in 1866. One suspects that, even to the Barrells, "Mt. Crawford" was a stretch. Before he let loose, though, Barrell donated one block to the Fire Department and discounted two to the Masons (who subsequently bought two more).

Portland has long been ambivalent about Lone Fir. At times it's embraced it and at times it has wanted to cut it loose. As noted, they didn't want to buy it at first, yet an 1877 fund drive collected $336.50 (which would be closer to $33,000 in today's money) towards clearing ground and providing wooden headboards where needed. In 1889 the city extended the Mt. Tabor trolley line to pass by the cemetery's portals. In 1903, five-hundred people contributed a total of $3500 for the erection of the Soldier's Monument in the cemetery.

Conditions slipped and by the 1920s voices were calling for the cemetery's dismantlement. Unfortunately for Lone Fir, the owners followed the common practice of the day of leaving cemetery upkeep to the individual plot owners. Inevitably, maintenance in such arrangements is uneven at best and the cemetery slowly became dilapidated.[12] Neighbors petitioned the government to discontinue use of the cemetery and remove the existing remains. In 1922 they modified their request in the form of proposed legislation, Senate Bill 102, to "prohibit further burials and turn the cemetery into a memorial park without disturbing the buried bodies"; a proposal successfully fought—much of it over the word "park"—by the Oregon Pioneer Association and the newly formed Lone Fir Cemetery Lot Owners' Association.

Nonetheless, matters did not improve and by the mid-1920s the Lone Fir Cemetery Lot Owners' Association effectively abandoned the cemetery. In 1928 the county threw in the towel and under state mandate accepted responsibility for maintaining Lone Fir and began its restoration. The county instituted a policy enforced until at least 1982 of having the cemetery open only during the week from 8 AM to 4 PM and closed on weekends when most people would be able to visit the graves of loved ones. A cemetery brochure from 1952 contains a list of rules which illuminates how differently the cemetery was perceived back then. Most noticeably, they admonish one to stay on the walks at all times and keep your pet on a leash. And for Pete's sake, don't let your under-sixteen-year old children wander the grounds unsupervised. Do not bother the birds or animals; no "refreshments, unless authorized by the management"; leave your bike or motorcycle outside the grounds; and no firearms, even if you don't shoot them. Along with loitering, "boisterous or unseemly conduct shall not be permitted in the Cemetery." No "improprieties," okay? And in case you're considering putting up a willy-nilly scarecrow or a blob of cement for your tombstone, be it noted that "any obnoxious or grotesque design will not be permitted."

BLOCK 14: THE CELESTIAL GARDEN

Rebecca Liu, a short, round-faced woman with an infectious enthusiasm, sat in a banquet room in her North Portland restaurant with fellow Chinese historian, Marcus Lee, a handsome man with a well trimmed goatee, and in two hours' time they gave me an introductory course in Chinese society in the guise of trying to unravel the history of Block 14.

Block 14 is one of thirty-nine (more or less) blocks in Lone Fir Cemetery. Block 14 was for many years reserved for the Chinese, until 1949 when the majority of the bones were removed and shipped to Hong Kong. Subsequent to their removal, Multnomah County built a works-building on the site, itself removed in 2007. Plans are in gear to convert what is now a vacant lot into a memorial park for the disinterred Chinese as well as the patients of a local psychiatric hospital, who were buried nearby.

Rebecca and Marcus were informally representing the CCBA, the Chinese Consolidated Benevolent Association, an organization founded in response to the Chinese Exclusion Act of 1882. Being of Norwegian extraction, I tend to think of the CCBA as the Sons of Norway on steroids. Not only do they stand as a bulwark for the Chinese in America, they protect their heritage, facilitate business, and foster Chinese-American communities. The CCBA organized the bone disinterment of 1949 (and the previous one) and is central to the planning and fund-raising for the memorial. Past principal of the CCBA Chinese School, Rebecca moved here from Taiwan in 1974. Marcus, CCBA archivist and museum director, is a Portland native whose great-great-grandfather, Lung Hing from Toisan, China, was a merchant in Chinatown. They represent the CCBA on the Lone Fir Foundation board.

Recently a 340-year old Chinese coin was dug up in the Yukon, one from roughly 1670. Such finds are more common on the coast, this one was unusually far inland. You can be pretty sure no Chinese were scouring the Yukon for beaver pelts at that time, but you know for sure that trading has always gone on everywhere.

The Chinese probably weren't on the coast, either, but the Russians may have been. Officially, they showed up in 1732 and didn't make landfall until 1741. But officialdom never ventures into the unknown; they head out to explore what they already know about. And Russia is a huge country; the tail doesn't necessarily know what the snout is sniffing. Certainly, the peoples on either side of the Bering Strait knew each other was there. They're not to be blamed if their capitals were somewhat out-of-touch. Likewise, you can be certain that trading ships were plying the Asian Pacific Coast since time immemorial, regardless of what the governments were doing. And if ships were sliding up the coast from Vladivostok seventy years before the Tsar took notice of Alaska, so be it. And if they found Chinese coins to be good trading stock, so be that, too. Japanese fisherman are known have have been washing up on the isles of B. C. since long before the Europeans showed up, so it's not unimaginable that some Chinese fishermen got blown over there, as well.

Be that as it may, the first noticeable group of Chinese showed up on the West Coast for the same reason most everyone else did: gold. Not in Portland, at first, but San Francisco. There's a good bet they were here within a year after the strike. Again, like everyone else, they followed the gold. And then the railroad. And then they had restaurants and laundries in every mining camp in the West. Within two years of the California strike, by 1850, Portland harbored the second largest Chinese community on the coast. It already had a Chinatown.

Whatever we know about that Chinatown, we know that people were dying there as soon as it sprang to life. Especially on the frontier, and it was a Chinese frontier as much as a Swede's. There is no record of a Chinese graveyard in Portland other than Lone Fir, although there had to have been a burial ground for them by 1850. Most likely, they were interred in one of the early pioneer graveyards long since abandoned and, hopefully, moved. On the other hand, we know that Lone Fir had its first guest in 1846 and, most likely, was accepting others in the early 1850s, prior to Colburn Barrell's purchase of it. An article in the *Sunday Oregonian* for May 1, 1887, suggests that "occasional interments [in Lone Fir] took place after 1850, but the grounds were not regarded as a general place of burial until probably about 1853 or 1854." Two years after that article, City & Suburban Railroad was contributing funds towards the Chinese section.

We can also pretty much assume that Seldon Murray paced off the original ten acres of the cemetery in 1846 when he agreed to let Emmor Stephens be buried there. If the Chinese started burying their community just outside the "official" cemetery walls prior to Barrell's involvement, it wouldn't surprise me. Nor would it surprise me if Barrell had made an agreement with someone from the Chinese community, by handshake, that they could use that land outside the cemetery, knowing that he was planning on buying and adding it to the cemetery soon, anyway. It was common in those days to wheel and deal land before one had proper title to it. Murray, for example, didn't officially receive his Donation Land Claim authorization until long after he'd sold much of it away, including that which went to Barrell.

Just who Barrell shook hands with is not recorded. The San Francisco branch of the Chinese Consolidated Benevolent Association began in 1882, and it sponsored the beginnings of the Portland branch in 1890, according to Ms Liu. Presumably, one of the "companies" which made up the CCBA was functioning as community spokesperson in Portland prior to that time.

The loss of the Chinese section in Lone Fir mirrors the loss of the Chinese community on the West Coast after the Chinese Exclusion Act of 1882. Aside from its greed and racial arrogance, excluding the Chinese tore a hole in the fabric of the community. An important part of the Portland tapestry was excised. A paragraph in D. A. Lund's c. 1928 paper,

"Lone Fir: Silent City of the Dead," guilelessly reports:

> The Chinese burial section embraces about an acre and was
> conferred without deed, by word of mouth alone. Some
> 300 are interred, *though no more Chinese funerals are permit-*
> *ted* [my emphasis]. Curious customs surrounded these
> pioneer Chinese burials. According to report each dead
> was given a coin to hold in the mouth, with which to pay
> admission to heaven—or perhaps it was to pay the ferry-
> man, Charon, to cross the Styx. All the deceased's papers
> were burnt in the brick oven... at the corner of the cem-
> etery acre. Food was provided and set out on the newly
> made grave so that the departed might not go hungry. In
> addition all the deceased's debts were paid—out of any
> estate left behind, or by relatives, friends or tong brethren,
> suggesting that in some cases, perhaps the dead had a
> shade best of the bargain.[13]

Lund, evidently, wasn't struck by the fact that "no more Chinese funerals are permitted"; which leaves one wondering
from where Percy Maddux got his description of a Chinese
funeral and when it took place, in his 1952 book, *City on the
Willamette*, where he describes an incident at one Chinese
funeral:

Upon arrival at the cemetery, fireworks were exploded and the coffin placed besides the grave, while candles were lighted and incense was made to waft its perfume on the air. The effects of the deceased were then gathered up to be burned. A bystander, thinking it a shame that a good musical instrument should be destroyed, seized a fiddle and tried to make off with it. He was pursued by several Chinese all the way to the edge of the cemetery, reaching which he threw the fiddle over the fence: but he did not fare so well himself. The Chinese caught him and held him until the instrument was recovered, after which they beat him with it until it was broken to pieces. They then returned to the fire and threw the pieces on it.[14]

None of this indicates when the Chinese returned to the good graces of the community and were once again allowed to be buried in Lone Fir. As far as I know, the exclusion was quietly forgotten.

The Chinese relationship with the American West is complex and unlike that of any other nationality. The Norwegians, Japanese, and Italians—forget about the Kenyans—never sent for the bones of their expatriates. Once they'd left the Mother Land, they were gone. Not so the Chinese. When the early Chinese came, they came expecting to return home someday, if not on their own two feet, then in a box. They didn't come to assimilate into America; they came to make money and go home.

Because of that expectation, the Chinese community here always considered itself a separate entity and has maintained its own enclaves in towns and governed its own affairs. It still does. In the late 19th and early 20th centuries, the bones of deceased Chinese were rounded up every score of years or so and shipped back to China. Except those of women and children.

The last time this happened was in 1948 and the county chipped in $715.20 towards metal boxes for some 265 remains.[15] In September of 1947, the CCBA was wrangling with the County over the County's contribution to the disinterment. A letter from the Park's Superintendent from then outlined the case:

> Negotiations have proceeded with the Chinese Benevolent Association and counter-proposals being offered whereby the County would bear the entire cost of removal and shipping. The proposal is obviously made for a bargaining basis as the Chinese Association is experiencing considerable

difficulty in raising funds to complete their portion of the operation. Their former estimates of the amounts of Christian Chinese for which graves would have to be provided has been raised from an estimated twelve in number not to exceed twenty. This proposal if accepted by Multnomah County would show an estimated cost as follows:

Cost of digging 250 graves, approximately	$500
Cost of furnishing graves for 20 Christian Chinese	$350
Cost of reburial of 20 Christian Chinese	$20
Cost of hiring a Chinese interpreter at $10 per day, approximately	$300
Cost of shipping to China 230 deceased Chinese	$3105
Total Estimated Cost	$4275

None of those estimates included cost for the boxes, and that's the only record of payment we have. Why the county would do that is contained in a earlier letter from the Superintendent to the Board: "In exchange the Chinese Association would consider releasing all claims to a plot of land known as the Chinese section of Lone Fir Cemetery of approximately 125 feet by 320 feet in size.... The cemetery has an urgent need of this parcel of ground for a building site

for shops."

In the end, it appears a good part of the exhumation and shipping costs were paid for by public subscriptions among the Chinese community stateside. The disinterments didn't happen only in Portland (which included Lincoln Memorial), they happened in Baker City, Coos Bay, Albany, Ontario, Ashland, Corvallis, Roseburg, The Dalles, Pendleton, and

Idaho, as well. All-in-all, ninety-three cases of bones from 600 individuals (265 from Lone Fir) were shipped aboard the Luxemboug Victory of the Pacific Far East line on July 5, 1949, for delivery to Tung Wah Hospital in Hong Kong, which was authorized to disperse them to their respective homes. Two years after shipment, in 1951, they were still sitting in a Hong Kong warehouse waiting for payment.

The Chinese Consolidated Benevolent Association, which was responsible for organizing the exhumation on the American end, had entrusted $2484.33 with one Fred K. Chinn (whose Chinese name was Foo Lin) of China Tradeways to arrange for the shipping, which he did. Only he forgot to pay for it, which was apparent when the boxes arrived in China. When confronted in October of 1949, he immediately produced two checks to cover the situation, which immediately bounced, beginning the long wait before the bones could get home. Chinn eventually did manage to come up with $941, but by this time wharfage charges had brought the total levy due to $3259.44 above what Chinn had paid. Frustrated, the CCBA finally went to the police and Chinn was arrested on May 7, 1951, with bail set at $10,000.

Less than two weeks later, the CCBA returned to court and said they'd changed their minds: they would assume responsibility for the fees and would like to drop any charges against Mr. Chinn. The court complied. The Chinese community would take care of its own.[16]

In 2009 an employee at Weiden+Kennedy in Portland, Ivy Lin, released a documentary about the contentious bones. She followed them all the way to Hong Kong. An undated article in *The Oregonian* reports:

> Lin's investigation took her to the Tung Wah Museum in Hong Kong, where she found records of the shipment—"I burst into tears," she said—and Tung Wah Coffin Home, a storage building where the remains are today.
>
> Or they maybe elsewhere—Lin said she thinks they may have been moved to a nearby cemetery. Even with letters of introduction from the benevolent association and officials from Metro, which runs Lone Fir, she had difficulty getting permission from Chinese authorities to pursue her search.

The CCBA plays a pivotal role in the Chinese community and has since the Chinese Exclusion Act of 1882. Different regions of the United States have different names for similar organizations. Portland follows the lead of San Francisco whose CCBA was an amalgam of the "six companies" in the aftermath of the act. The companies were, it is my understanding, a combination of district and surname organiza-

Proposed
Heritage & Memorial Garden

Block 14 was for many years the traditional burying ground of Portland's Chinese until that responsibility was handed to Lincoln Memorial Park in the 1900s. Negotiations and control over Block 14 (southwest corner of the cemetery) were vague until the exhumation of the Chinese bones in 1949 and their subsequent return to China. After that, the county took control of land and built an office building/shop there, which was removed in 2007. As it turned out, some of the bones were missed and the situation was complicated by the near-by burial of some 132 anonymous patients from the Hawthorne Asylum. In an evolution of concerns over proper memorialization of those groups, a consortium of the Friends of Lone Fir, the Chinese Consolidated Benevolent Association, and Metro developed a plan for a memorial garden on Block 14.

The Lone Fir Foundation grew out of that consortium as a way to fund both the Heritage & Memorial Garden and further restoration and renovation of the cemetery.

SE Morrison Street

SE 20th Avenue

tions and were already cooperating prior to the act. Exactly what these organizations do is difficult for Americans to grasp. As organizations, they act as governments and banks in absentia for the Chinese community abroad, not just in America but in places such as Australia and the Philippines, as well. During the heyday of Chinese immigration, they recruited emigrants, arranged for their passage, met them at the dock, and provided them with homes and jobs, as well as providing loans and sending money back to the mainland. For the most part, they are groups of people with a

common interest, either they hail from the same district or they share a last name. In a country like ours with hundreds of thousands of surnames, it's hard to imagine the Smiths all getting together and finding each other jobs and lending themselves money; but China has many fewer last names, and, obviously, a different way of counting relations than we do. Surnames in China more resemble clan names or association names where a person adopts a name to be associated with a particular person or family, and doesn't necessarily represent blood relationship; not unlike the European system where an occupational surname such as Smith doesn't imply consanguinity. Still, whereas in America similar surnames can mean mere coincidence, in China it means social relationship. And the groupings can be sizable. Nearly eight percent of the people in mainland China, for example, are of the Li/Lee clan. In Portland the Lee clan is planning on erecting their own headquarters aided by the San Francisco branch of the "family."

In any event, these family associations along with regional associations banned together in the wake of the Exclusion Act to form the CCBA and lobby on behalf of the general Chinese population. These groupings are not to be confused with the tongs, which spring from the same ground and operate similarly, some illegal behavior notwithstanding.[17]

The County administration building, since taken over by Metro, didn't last long into the twenty-first century when it was torn down clearing the southwest section of the cemetery once again. By 2007 Metro had agreed to participate in turning the area into a park commemorating both the Chinese and the inmates of Dr. Hawthorne's asylum for the impaired, some 132 (by some counts) of whom are buried in Lone Fir anonymously. The idea is not new; a 1920s brochure from the Lone Fir Cemetery Lot Owners Association suggested turning the Chinese section into a park.

The Resurrection

Lone Fir wasn't the only cemetery dropped in the county's lap. They added Multnomah Park (82nd Ave. and Holgate) in 1944 and between then and 1971 they added eleven more.[18] None of them did they seek out. The value of this to the cemeteries was immense. If nothing else, deterioration was at least slowed down. From now on, someone would cut the grass and stand the vandalized tombstones up-right again. The cemeteries began a long period of hibernation. The modern era began in 1994 when Multnomah County handed their parks and cemeteries over to the newly formed regional government, Metro.

Metro had no idea what to do with them. They were an irksome adjunct to their parks and green spaces, except that they were not quite either, yet both. Their first reaction was to try and get rid of them. They weren't really parks, after all, they were ongoing businesses. They were a park like a baseball field is a park: someone has to pay for it. The users. So why not just sell the cemeteries to someone already in the business?

Which was a good theory except that no one wanted to buy them. Fourteen scattered, mostly tiny cemeteries in need of work were impossible to peddle; so with the millennium drawing to a close, Metro bit the bullet and began considering what to do with their baby. Can't kill it; can't throw it out with the bath water; might as well figure out how to raise it up.

What was first apparent was that cemeteries, indeed, were not like other parks and green spaces but rather needed their own special care and attention; care and attention that was, in theory, provided by perpetual care funds, of which there were none. Nor were their sufficient funds in the maintenance budget for anything beyond basic mainte-

nance. Restoration and repair would have to wait for special funding.[19] The effect was to slide the cemeteries toward the lap of the Director of Volunteer Services for Metro's Parks and Greenspaces, who at the time was the young, delightfully named Lupine Hudson.

Although Lupine was living just a couple of blocks from Lone Fir when she was handed over responsibility for rounding up support for it, she'd never stepped foot inside the fences. Once she did, she realized she'd been missing a special space with enormous potential. She wasn't of the age where cemeteries were yet on her horizon, but she threw herself into finding support for the hallowed grounds.

She did it by culling workers from her existing volunteer staff at Metro and advertising the need on Metro's website and newsletter. She expanded to the Buckman Neighborhood Association and across the street to Central Catholic High. She began a monthly cleanup day. Monthly cleanup days meant public exposure; visitors to the cemetery asked what they were doing; more people volunteered.

Then people started to ask about who was buried there. Slowly, monthly work days morphed into monthly work and tour days. Problem was, no one had a handle on the history. No one had pulled together the story of either the place or its residents. Furthermore, the needs of restoration and protection went far beyond what the county could supply. It became evident that the volunteers had to be organized into their own group; one that could set its own agenda and generate its own funds. With Metro's encouragement and oversight, to be sure.[20]

In 2000 the volunteers reconstituted themselves as the Friends of Lone Fir and began their own program of restoration and development. They began repairing stones and organizing tours and events. The cemetery was opened all week round and increased its public profile. The Friends worked to get the cemetery included on the National Registry of Historic Places. Local musicians produced a CD on its behalf. Movies, TV shows, and music videos began being filmed there. Between all the new attention and the influx of Easter European tombstone styles, Lone Fir assumed a vitality it never before achieved.

The Friends also spearheaded the modern movement towards erecting a memorial park where the Chinese cemetery used to be; which in turn spurred the formation of the Lone Fir Foundation, promoted by Metro as a means of receiving larger grants and donations.

It would be hard to overestimate Metro's role in the transformation of Lone Fir. Begrudging acceptance has turned into embracement. From trying to dump the properties, the cemetery office staff has grown to four people. In 2011 under the guidance of current director, Rachel Fox, Metro commissioned an exhaustive inventory of all it cemeteries, the *Operations Assessment & Financial Planning Report,* with the aim of determining what has to be done to preserve the status quo while looking toward how to pay for the future. Freedom is not the only thing not free; add history to the list.

Realistically, the cemeteries will never pay for themselves; if they could, they would have been snapped up when offered, but that didn't happen. None of the cemeteries came into Metro's hands with perpetual endowment funds. There will never be enough new interments to create an endowment fund sufficient to maintain them. Which doesn't mean that strategies can't be employed to generate greater operating funds; which, essentially, is what Metro is looking at: how to increase revenue.

Lone Fir's ability to generate funds is increasingly limited, particularly, due to plot sales being curtailed; selling-out is always a threat. Eventually, further open plots will be found and a few interments permitted, but unless new ground can be found, that avenue is closing. One avenue for new ground would be to decommission some of the roadways within the cemetery and turn them into burial plots, but the roads themselves are part of the historical features of the cemetery and not necessarily available for change. A more possible avenue is through columbaria where cremains are stored above ground. With better than 70% of Oregonians opting for cremation these days, it's a viable choice. One task will be convincing people who choose cremation that having a memorial spot is crucial for the people left behind.

That Fox's position exists at all is indicative of Metro's increasing sensitivity to its peculiar parks. When Metro assumed control of the fourteen cemeteries in 1994, they were managed by two people, which included the park ranger, the on-the-ground maintenance person. Currently, five people do the work along with scores of volunteers. What was once a liability is now a tourist attraction.

The culmination of the attention was a listing of Lone Fir by *National Geographic Traveler* in fall of 2011 as one of the "ten best cemeteries in the world to visit." Admittedly, the phrase "to visit" leaves a lot of wiggle room and I know there are scores of cemeteries around the country, much less the world, that think they should have been included before Lone Fir; but it has the luxury of being above the fray: it's on the list.

So, why did Lone Fir make the list? Two reasons: cachet and J. B. Stephens. Cachet because Portland has enjoyed at least two decades worth of favorable national publicity. A) We aren't sure why; but B) we think it's well deserved. We're pretty smug. Regardless, that national infatuation with the town gives us higher standing than we, perhaps, deserve. It's okay, we can handle it.

But we know J.B. was important, he set the tone. He not only started the place, he knew that when he died he wasn't destined for an imaginary kingdom in the sky; he was heading "back to the elements of the universe, of which we were first composed." He was a kindly and practical realist who visited his wife's grave daily until his own demise. He was satisfied being a part of the grand and endless universe. Thanks to his wisdom, Lone Fir became a haven for Free-thinkers and the Enlightenment. This cemetery belongs to Mother Nature; like the state, she flies with her own wings.

SOME BACKGROUND

Cemeteries are not a new idea. Half of archaeology is digging up old cemeteries. The Pyramids are cemeteries. The Taj Mahal is a cemetery. Stonehenge is a cemetery. For all we know, your backyard is a cemetery; bones show up every-where. Prior to the 19th century, cemeteries, in European/American tradition, were primarily the responsibility of the family, the church, or the municipality.

The modern cemetery was invented in France in the early 1800s and was quickly adopted stateside at Mt. Auburn Cemetery in Cambridge, Massachusetts. Most histories of American cemeteries concentrate on the design influence of Mt. Auburn and the "rural" or "garden" cemetery move-ment; but as or more important for America was the intro-duction of the concept that anyone could open a cemetery. In America the design concept was often ignored or bas-tardized, but the business model took firm hold. In America death became a business and, for the most part, municipali-ties today only operate abandoned pioneer cemeteries such as Metro's fourteen.

Lone Fir is a classic example of the iconic Oregon pioneer graveyard: the Donation Land Claim (DLC) cemetery. It's been said that the Oregon Trail is the longest cemetery in the world, which illustrates the reality that people have been dying here since before they got here. Some of the pre-Euroamerican Oregonians had cemeteries, but didn't bury their dead, as they do now.[21] The missionaries established cemeteries as did some communities before legal title could be secured; but a good many of the pioneer cemeteries still in existence began when someone on a new DLC kicked the bucket and had to be planted somewhere. Often as not, that somewhere was the back forty. Once someone was in the ground, when the next person died—even if it was a neigh-bor—the logical place to stick him or her was next to the other newly departed so as to have company. Bingo; one's a gravesite, two's a cemetery.

Lone Fir begins when Seldon Murray's neighbor's dad was buried on the northwest corner of his claim. He was a nice guy, that Seldon. One stiff was enough for Seldon to rope off ten acres for a cemetery, the ten he sold to Barrell. He even declared the ten acres a cemetery and sold it before he had legal title to it himself; processing DLCs was slow. Exactly who Murray originally thought was going to run this cemetery is not known, but he seems to have grabbed at Barrell's offer to take it off his hands. Buy it, even. I sus-pect Barrell thought all along that the city would buy the cemetery off him, because cities ran cemeteries; that's what they'd always done. Not this time, though. By this time, towns and cities were getting out of the cemetery business; it was being taken over by private enterprise. Fortunately, Barrell quickly found other buyers and Lone Fir survived.

Until it floundered into neglect and was rescued by state action and impassioned pleas from the sons and daughters of the pioneers. It's a history oft repeated throughout the state. It's one of the virtues of Lone Fir, its uniqueness yet its commonality. Other cemeteries may have their elegance and propriety, Lone Fir has the state's soul. Yet it fearfully illustrates the problems of commercialized death: when a cemetery turns unprofitable, who's going to keep it up?

You and me, that's who.

NOTES

[1] These old newspaper columns are bound into scrapbooks maintained in the Oregon Historical Society library.

[2] *Multnomah County Record of Deeds, Book G*, pg.307.

[3] In fact, Joseph Barrell accompanied Gray on the 1792 voyage. J. Barrell, according to the media series *Hit and Run History* (WGBH Boston), was a Boston grocer who rose from being in the bottom 30 percentile of wealthy Americans to being in the top 1% due to two circumstances: one, he was appointed as a privateer during the Revolutionary War; and, two, thanks to a proficiency in French he secured the contract for supplying the French fleet as it sat in Boston Harbor. J. Barrell had three wives (not at once) and twenty children (not at once, either). Another sponsor of the voyage, C. Hatch, was a slave trader.

[4] Records in the Multnomah County Records Dept. show Barrell at some point buying property from the heirs of Crawford Dobbins. They also show Barrell buying a considerable amount of property in a relatively short time.

[5] *Sunday Oregonian*, May 1, 1887.

[6] "Situated on the north west corner of said Murray claim and containing ten square acres in the form of a square orig. six hundred and sixty feet equal sides...." *Book A*, pg. 94, *Mult. Co. Deeds*. Murray's first name is occasionally spelled "Selden."

[7] MSS 1275, *Abstract of Deeds 1855-1858*, Multnomah County. This book also contains another abstract of the Murray/Barrell deed which formally began the cemetery. The primary difference between the accounts is that this manuscript gives the measurements in rods, forty equalling 660 feet. Where I have inserted the word "north" into this abstract, the original document reads "south,' whereas a reading of the document makes the error clear. I reproduce punctuation, grammar, and spelling as I find them.

[8] Murray's land claim wasn't officially registered until 1862, by which time he'd been selling chunks of the claim for years.

[9] The best history of Lone Fir and source of much of this material is an article from the *Sunday Oregonian*, May 1, 1887. It is one of the few histories to get the land purchases correct. Being the history written closest to the time frame helps. Some histories repeat the facts correctly but then ignore what they've written and adopt the theory of Barrell buying land from Stephens. The deeds from the crucial late 1860s years are missing.

[10] Op cit. *Book A*.

[11] In referring to James "Pappy" Stephens' ferry, a Portland newspaper of July 28, 1851, commented: "At first this craft was hand-propelled by Indian paddlers, but later it was mule-powered by means of a mule walking in a treadle. Eventually it became known at the Stark street ferry."

[12] "Dilapidate" comes from the Latin *dilapidare*, meaning "to scatted apart stone-by-stone"; an appropriate cemetery word.

[13] D. A. Lund is the *nom de plume* of Charles Oluf Olson. The paper is available in several copies at both the State Historical Society and Metro's offices. It is one of the sources for errors about the early history of the cemetery.

[14] My quotes came from mimeographed copies of the book in among the files at OHS and Metro.

[15] While, according to a letter in Metro files from Parks Superintendent Syverson to the Multnomah County Board, "The remains of the deceased Chinese were removed from Lone Fir Cemetery as of July 21, 1948…; a total of 265 deceased persons were removed exclusive of children where no remains could be found"; the permits to "disinter, remove and reinter remains of several hundred deceased Chinese" weren't authorized until June 8, 1949.

[16] Most of this information comes from *The Oregonian*, May 9, 1951 and May 22, 1951, available online; the rest is from the *Oregon Journal*, July 8, 1948, available in the "Vertical Files, Lone Fir Cemetery," at the Oregon Historical Society. The eventual disposition of the bones is still unknown.

[17] Some of this information was extracted from Wikipedia. Ms Liu and Mr. Lee are not responsible for any errors; they're all mine.

[18] Jones Cemetery had belonged to Multnomah County since 1872 when its founder, Nathan B. Jones, sold it to a county judge for $1.

[19] When the state mandated that the county take over Lone Fir in 1928, they added a clause allowing the county to raise designated cemetery funds through a tax levy. There has been debate through the years over whether or not this is still applicable. The final word has not been spoken; it could well be revisited in the future.

[20] Conversations with Ms Hudson and Rachel Fox, Manager of Metro Cemetery Program, supplied the bulk of this information.

[21] Native American cemeteries in this region are an amalgam of Euroamerican and native practices. They have adopted below ground burials, but they retain native decorative/offering customs. In this region, most tribes used some form of above ground burial, frequently by placing the bodies in canoes held above ground on supports. After the arrival of the Euroamericans, they learned to smash holes in the bottoms of these canoes, otherwise the Euroamericans would steal them.

Macleay Mausoleum

DONALD MACLEAY WAS A SCOTSMAN via Canada who at a young age made a bundle off shipping, banking, exporting, and assorted other ventures. Aside from the mausoleum, he's famous for donating the first major park to the city of Portland, Macleay Park, now a part of Forest Park. Portland Parks and Rec says the original owner of the Macleay Park land, one Danford Balch, was a "peaceful man" who happened to blow both sides of a double-barrel shotgun into the chest of Mortimer Stump who had eloped with his daughter. Despite claiming it as an accident, he was hung in front of a crowd of 500 people, entertainment being limited in those days.

According to Parks and Rec, "Macleay, a Scotsman, gave the land to the city in 1897 in commemoration of the 60th anniversary of Queen Victoria's reign, but that was not the only reason! It is said that Macleay complained that his taxes on the property were too high and that he would rather give his land to the city for park purposes than pay so much in taxes. The Deputy Assessor, L. S. Maxwell, countered with, 'Well, then, why don't you?' Macleay returned to the courthouse three days later with a deed turning the steep, rough gulch of tall timbers into Macleay Park."

By far the grandest mausoleum in the state, the Gothic Macleay Mausoleum built in 1877 at a cost of $13,500 suffers from decades of neglect and weathering. Stones have fallen from the facade and more threaten. Estimates to restore it range around the one million dollar mark. Despite its disrepair, or maybe because of it, it is a favorite location for movies, TV shows, and music videos. It's not true that Gus van Sant used to sleep in the crypt.

Notable Monuments

Numbers refer to block and lot numbers; e.g. Block 3, Lot 215 is written 3.215.

1.1 *Crawford Dobbins*: Tall obelisk has on its east face a carving of a truncated pine tree with eight spreading branches (the cover of this book), reminiscent of a Japanese crest. The elegance of the design contrasts with the brutalism of the concrete. It was an auspicious beginning to the cemetery; Crawford was the second person officially buried here.

1.18 *James and Eliza Stephens*: Three-quarters life-size, almost full relief, carvings of the founders of the cemetery; it was J. B.'s father who was the first burial. It is their epitaph about "nature's immutable laws" that set the tone for Lone Fir.

2.16 *W. H. Frush*: Large marble bowl with the face of a bon vivant as the spout. This used to be removed each New Years for mixing Tom & Jerrys and then returned. It has since been cemented down.[1]

3.215 *Elizabeth Miller*: Flat stone with a line-engraving of, I presume, the author of the accompanying poem:

Folks in Heaven don't do a thing
Walk streets of gold, play harp & sing
I need a little house, flowers round the door
Children running in & out to bake some cookies for
Save your golden streets for those up above
Satisfy my simple tastes with lots of folks to love

3.219 *Thomas Dryer*: Red granite upright has a simplistic carving of an early building housing *The Oregonian* offices, erected for "Editor of the first/ weekly *Oregonian*." An anti-slavery Whig, Dryer was the first known person to have climbed Mt. Hood.

4.68 *Ivan Salazar*: Upright stone cut in the shape of a Teddy Bear. It may not be high art, but it's noticeable, kid-friendly and a sign of the times.

5 *The Firemen's Plot*. Donated by Barrell to the firemen. Has its own plotting and centers around a flag pole.

6.82 *George Bottler*: Small mausoleum for the second commercial brewer in the city, who eventually sold out to Henry Weinhard. In the process of being restored.

6M.3A *Frederic Roeder*: Thin upright with an engraving of an empty boat on a raging sea; in the foreground, a pair of hands thrust up from the water. Drowned, indeed.

7M.30 *Helen & Dale Jones*: A granite bench accompanied
by a small sarcophagus. The bench is inscribed with
the memorable epitaph: "This wasn't in my schedule
book." The other edge says, "Keep your chins up."
They liked to eat.

8.18 *Sara Holzman*: Lengthy poem by Robinson Jeffers on a
large slab.

[To the Stone-Cutters]

Stone-cutters
    fighting time with marble,
    you foredefeated
Challengers of Oblivion
Eat cynical earnings,
    knowing rock splits,
    records fall down,
The square-limbed
    Roman letters
Scale in the thaws,
    wear in the rain.
    The poet as well
Builds his monument mockingly:
For man will be blotted out,
    the blithe earth die,
    the brave sun
Die blind
    and blacken to the heart:
Yet stones have stood
    for a thousand years,
    and pained thoughts found

The honey of peace in old poems.
R.[obinson] J.[effers] 1924

8.59 *Benjamin Morris*: A particularly handsome ledger stone in dark gray. The layout is restrained and the font, reminiscent of William Morris, is delicious: "Be doers of the Word and not hearers only." The good man was a bishop of Oregon and Washington.

8.86 *Harriet Rodney*: An unusual low sarcophagus surmounted by a lengthy cross that looks all the world like a sword from the Knights Templar; surely the Sword of the Lord.

8M.44 *James Hawthorne*: Elaborate obelisk. Hawthorne was the psychiatrist who ran the Hawthorne Asylum at the east end of Hawthorne Avenue. One-hundred-thirty-two anonymous inmates of that institution are buried in or near Block 14.

8M.61 Three Russian teenagers killed in a fire share neighboring, black granite monuments with laser-etched portraits. The graves are always well tended and florid. There is an eerily similar trio of graves in Redmond Memorial Cemetery.

8M.74 *Tony Riggs*: A stark, black square pedestal topped with a sundial face sans gnomon (the upright piece which casts the shadow), bearing a French inscription: *"L'heure passe, l'amitié rest"*; "The hour passes, friendship remains."

8M.246 *Leslie Hansen/Eric Ladd*: Unquestionably one of the more interesting monuments in Lone Fir, this grave is surrounded by an ornate, cast-iron fence, the only one of its kind in the cemetery. Within the fence, embedded in a concrete slab, is an equally ornate, cast-iron, supine cross. Né Leslie Hansen, he adopted Eric Ladd as a stage name and was "the father of historic preservation" in town. The cast-iron fencing came from Mark Twain's Albany, NY home.

9.79 *Chris & Hope Carter*: Upright noticeable not for its face but for its verso, which is covered with a reproduction of Gustav Klimt's "The Kiss," with the inexplicable addition of a pair of hand and foot prints at the bottom.

9M.22 *Maureen Rahman*: Large, black granite upright with a chunk taken out of a corner. It bears a quote from Victor Hugo: "Oh, the love of a mother, / love which none can forget."

9M.219 *Diana Holzhausen & Patrick Moxhet*: Large, patterned granite block carved on all four sides. Quotes, etching, and enigmas. Who is carrying the trident and the bow?

11.3 Upright memorial stone to the unknown Japanese buried here, faced with three Japanese characters.

12.79 *Elenor Springer*: Stele with well preserved, delicate filigree carvings surrounding a hand holding deeply carved roses, from 1880.

12.211 *Phillipa & Richard Harrison*: Gray granite upright with an eloquent epitaph for Phillipa:

> Where there was hate, she sowed love;
> Where there was injury, pardon;
> Where there was doubt, faith;
> Where there was darkness, light;
> Where there was sorrow, joy.

This tombstone is usually topped with remembrance pebbles.

13.22 *Sam Simpson*: Large upright fronted by a granite bench. "Oregon poet/ Author of 'Beautiful Willamette,'" from which a verse is excerpted:

> Onward ever,
> Lovely river,
> Softly calling to the sea,
> Time, that scars us
> Maims and mars us,
> Leaves no track or trench on thee.

16.7 *Elsie Perry*: Modest, red granite pillow with an endearing epitaph:

Born in the country
Raised in the sticks

16.29 *Vera Shevchuk*: Arguably, the most elegant of the modern monuments, this is made of rough-formed concrete with a steel name plate. Formed of two upright slabs and a planter extension, it appears to be a cross between Frank Lloyd Wright's Falling Water and Le Corbusier. It was built in situ.

16.35 *Ernest Bonner*: New obelisks are a rarity. This polished, black granite one is from 2004.

17.2 New door on small brick building behind MacLeay Mausoleum, notable for its pineapple-themed hinge plates.

17.3 *MacLeay Mausoleum*: Grandest mausoleum in the state, built in 1877 for $13,500, it contains a small chapel which used to be open for public use during inclement weather.

17.5.C&G *A. G. & Cynthis Cunningham*: Collapsed vaults with end stones still standing. Vaults were sometimes erected over graves to prevent grave robberies, although it's not known if that was the intent here. At one time there used to be "grave bombs" available that would explode if hit with a shovel.

18.1.H *George & Margaret Otay*: A pair of the most unusual headstones in the cemetery; these are thin, hand-poured steles with rounded tops that look ever so much like the temporary headstones people erect in their yards at Halloween. One expects to see artificial spider-webbing draped over them. Lettering hand-inscribed and fairly random. One stone is inscribed with a small patch to look like exposed brick. I'm not convinced their last name is Otay, but what do I know?

18.6.D *Fannie Hamshaw*: Stocky, square, red-granite pillar with an unattributed epitaph from Henry Wadsworth Longfellow, the second verse of the poem "The Reaper and The Flowers":

"Shall I have nought that is fair?" saith he;
"Have nought but the bearded grain?
Though the breath of these flowers is sweet to me,
I will give them all, back again."

18.208 *Constance Olds*: Largish upright with a photoceramic and a reverse covered in black hand-prints; plus an old bromide for an epitaph:

We love you a bushel
And a peck and a peck
Around the neck

19.231 *Julius Ceasar*: A modest headstone for an old Negro League baseball player who left us with his favorite shout-out: "Play ball"! No, his last name is not misspelled. At least not according to this Julius. (Although I'd never rule out a typo.)

20.39 *Shawn Miller*: This dramatic, laser-etched, black granite upright has the deceased's portrait surrounded by a billow of dust coming from a drag racer at the bottom of the stone. NHRA championship decals are etched into the upper corners. Maybe the best part is that Mr. Miller is a dead-ringer (oops!) for David Crosby. "Gone home to horsepower heaven."

20.23(A) *Joel Weinstein*: skeleton riding a bike accompanied by a skeleton pig. In color against black granite. Mr. Weinstein, who currently has a peyote pot sitting by the headstone, was touring in Puerto Rico when he passed.

22.16 *Wheeler*: Granite cube inscribed with names on the sides.

22.19 *Donald Johnson*: Flat - a cryptic epitaph that leaves one wondering: "From childhood's hour I have not/ been as others were."

22.203 *Jason Hatfield:* Tall stele with an excerpt from *Romeo and Juliet*:

> …and, when he shall die,
> take him and cut him out
> in little stars
> and he will make the face
> of heaven so fine
> that all the world will be
> in love with the night
> and pay no worship
> to the garish sun.

25.13 *Rosalinda Alfaro:* A curved, handmade "adobe" stone backing a Jesus-bearing cross. I'm sure this graceful tombstone is supposed to be outside a mission in New Mexico. Catch it when the light dapples its face. Bring a rose for *Día de los Muertos*.

25.72 *Paul Lind:* The oft-photographed "star" of the new monuments is this life-size reproduction, in full color, of a Scrabble board. The choice of words is intensely personal. The seven letters in the "player's" hand: WEMISSU.

26.30 *Minh & Mary Tran*: This polished, black granite ball is engraved with Asian dragons and rests on a cubic granite socket. If that weren't enough, the names are enigmatic. In large font, above their "real" names, are the names EJ & PJ Dragonhorn.

26.40 *The Rose Garden*. The Rose Garden. The roses are all heritage. Of humble proportions but lovingly tended as deserves the city's iconic flower, it began in 1943 when

Portland's Pioneer Rose Association planted cuttings from twenty-three rose species brought west on the Oregon Trail.

28.3 *Maxine McCloskey*: A natural stone—which is rare in this cemetery—for a lady who spent her life advocating for whales. It carries a whale engraving and a heartfelt epitaph:

She lived so that the wild creatures
of the earth
including those in the ocean's depths
would want to bless her.

30.40 *David Lesman*: Another natural stone; this one has two fish carved into it as well as a fisherman (presumably David) and three trees. David has "Gone fishin'." He has lots of company.

34.5 *Mary Kennan & Lisette Stephens*: Austere, short-armed concrete cross. It's modest but powerful in its simplicity. "Of such is the kingdom of heaven."

34.273 *Jesus Morales*: Handmade mosaic—white shards against black grout—cross on a mosaic pedestal. There are not a lot of mosaics in the cemetery; this is a standout.

36.23 *Michael Parker*: This upright carries two brass-covered photoceramics. Michael was developmentally challenged, but his parents have erected a very positive and loving memorial to their son. It is both painful and reassuring. There is a lot of text associated with this headstone.

36.78 *Donald (Duck) Collins*: Hard to miss this small upright upon entering Lone Fir from the east. The engraving of the race car in front of the crossed victory leaps out at the passer-by. You might want to contrast this with Shawn Miller's NHRA championship stone.

37.1 *Jess Nudsen*: This small, elaborate upright sitting next to the road has a barely noticeable epitaph carved into a lower face. It is as evocative an epitaph as there is in the cemetery, or anywhere, for that matter:

Some where, some time,
We'll understand.

38.69(A) *John & Alta Haelen*: This polished black granite, slanting upright has a laser etching of the couple on the front. The rear credits John with being "one of the foremost magazine 'illustrators in the country,'" and is enlivened by a laser etching of, one presumes, one of his illustrations.

38.292 *Joan Almasan*: A handmade, concrete monument reminiscent of Rosalinda Rosario's altar-like marker, this has painted lettering and the design of two palm trees on a tiny island. In the center a blank square is outlined as if waiting for a portrait.

D.10 *Fried Egger*: this flush stone might be a tad hard to find, and perhaps just knowing that it's there is sufficient; but it's hard to pass up for the name alone. Hear tell his brother was a poacher.

Milepost P2

In 1851 THE GODS OF ARBITRATION decided that a point in the West Hills above Portland was the best spot from which to divide up the state. The spot had to be south of the Columbia River and west of Lake Vancouver (which many people don't even know exists) while staying to the east of the Columbia where it bends north. Shortly thereafter, a road, now Stark Street, was cut due east along that line to the Sandy River. Beginning downtown at the county courthouse a stone milepost was erected for each mile all the way to the Sandy, fifteen in all. Each had its surface hand-cut with a "P" for "Portland," and a number corresponding to it's mileage from the courthouse. Of the original fifteen, nine survive, one encased in the north wall of Lone Fir (accessible from the sidewalk outside the cemetery). They are some of the earliest public monuments extant in the city.

Who erected them is unknown though it's suspected they were put up by an Army garrison quartered downtown.

Heritage Rose Garden

IT SHOULD PROBABLY BE CALLED the Mary Drain Albro Heritage Rose Garden, as Ms Albro was key to its inception. As one might suspect, she is a descendant of the Drains who founded the eponymous town along Elk Creek in Douglas County. It was she who in 1936 founded the Pioneer Rose Association, and it was she who organized the ladies to scour the Oregon Territory from Walla Walla to the Applegate Valley for scions of roses brought across the plains by pioneering women. They found twenty-three. It was she who intertwined forever the image of the rose and the pioneers. The motto of the association reads: "With the Bible, the Flag, and the Rose, they built the Empire." She neglected to mention the "germs, guns, and steel."

Ms Albro planted five heritage rose gardens, with Lone Fir's, dating from 1943, being the only one still standing (others were in Champoeg, Forest Grove, Salem, and Walla Walla). Through the years, some of the rose varieties in this garden have been lost, but efforts are underway to restore what can be restored and to eventually landscape it. As it is, it remains a living tie with the indomitable women who brought their homes with them across the prairies.

THE MARKERS

COLBURN BARRELL IS CREDITED in most histories as being the founder of Lone Fir, although that honor rightfully belongs to J. B. Stephens. According to Wikipedia, Stephens was a cooper and shop-keeper from the Midwest who brought his wife, Elizabeth—with whom he had seven children—and his father with him to Portland.[1] Photographs of him show a man with a longer, thinner face than what appears on his tombstone, but still wearing his accustomed "Amish" beard sans mustache. His dad, buried upon Seldon Murray's land claim, was the first burial in Lone Fir; and it was Stephens who wrung the promise from Murray to keep it a cemetery. For that alone, we can be thankful to James and Elizabeth.

But their importance goes far beyond that, they set the tone for the cemetery. Not only did they erect a magnificent sculpture bearing their likenesses, but they chiseled out the epitaph that declared Lone Fir, not just sacred, but liberated ground, as well. They weren't counting on heaven, seeing a savior, or sitting at the right hand of God. No amorphous, mythical kingdom for them; they were "awaiting nature's immutable laws to return us back to the elements of the universe, of which we were first composed." Carl Sagan couldn't have said it better.

Colburn Barrell likewise eschewed God when he erected an obelisk to his best friend, Crawford Dobbins, eponym for the first cemetery iteration. He adorned it with a seal of a truncated cedar with spreading branches. Portland didn't have pious beginnings, and it's appropriate that its premier pioneer cemetery welcomed the hoi polloi along with *la haute société*. In the 1940s D. A. Lund wrote:

The ancient half of Lone Fir conveys a lesson in the democracy the pioneers not only believed in but lived. Here is no rank of any sort. All nations are represented, all grades of society, all states of wealth and standing. Rich lie here and poor, employer and employee, important and nondescript, those of virtue and those without. Here rests the sinner and the saint, the criminal and the judge. Here are graves of parsons, saloonkeepers, vagrants, gamblers and street walkers. Death has a way of banishing snobbishness, of cultivating comradeship. When women from houses of ill fame died, their sort of friends saw that they had a decent burial – the tinhorns, bartenders, madams and others. This is a matter of record. As to nationalities – almost every country has its son or daughter, including the Japanese. Only the Chinese have a corner of their own – the extreme southwest.[2]

There may be a few less murderers and ladies of the night buried there these days, but it's still a colorful and eccentric crew. Take note of the Scrabble board, the bike-riding skeleton, the drag racer, the dragon ball. Even the largest, ostensibly Christian symbol in the entire cemetery, the lyrical Celtic cross, is as much Irish as Catholic, replacing the body of Christ with roses, thistles, and ivy leaves.

Cemeteries are excellent repositories of the past because they rarely get makeovers. Nobody comes in and says let's put a new facade on that tombstone. No one suggests putting a new coat of paint on that statue. What you erect—minus weathering—is what you get. If your era is Victorian froufrou, Victorian froufrou is what you get. If your era is the Man in the Gray Flannel Suit, your tombstone will say Man in the Gray Flannel Suit. If your marker is from today, it's likely to have a photo-ceramic of your Harley and an etching of your dog, Schuster.

But the history hiding in a cemetery is more than mere style. Much of how a people see themselves, how they arrange themselves, is reflected in how they remember their dead, of which levels of ostentation are only one index. Some cultures—Scandinavian, for example—frown on excessive displays at death, so their cemeteries tend to be devoid of the noticeable differentiation which occurs in American graveyards. In Lone Fir one can contrast the grandiose MacLeay Mausoleum with the hand-poured, hand-scratched lettering of the Otay concrete steles. One can appreciate the Scandinavian sentiment while decrying the curtailing of information that happens in such an ethos.

That the Masons bought four blocks of Lone Fir speaks to their former importance in the community. Often they carved out entire cemeteries by themselves, such as Columbia Pioneer out on Sandy and Killingsworth. The only hint remaining of them in Lone Fir is the occasional square and compasses, which signifies their order, gracing a tombstone, and in the letter "M" included in certain block numbers on Lone Fir plot maps. Another commonly seen symbol on older tombstones are the three links of the Odd Fellows' chain meaning friendship, love, and truth. The Odd Fellows were even more diligent than the Masons in establishing cemeteries, in Oregon at a rate of nearly two-to-one. Far down the line are the Knights of Pythias, but they, too, occasionally cobbled together a cemetery.

The former importance of fraternal organizations in everyday American life shouldn't be overlooked. In many ways they functioned as a secondary church, as a social gathering place, a benefit organization, and a moral force in the community, as well as a source of galas and holiday entertainments. Much of their early strength came as insurance organizations for their members, and some of them devolved into being primarily that. One such group, the Woodmen of the World (WOW), for quite some time included tombstone money in their death benefits: $100.[3] The amount never changed, so that in time it lost much of its value to inflation; but nonetheless, the period around the turn of the 19th to the 20th century produced many a tombstone with the WOW axe, maul, and log chiseled onto its face. In Lone Fir that number is sixty-seven.

The WOW are responsible for the majority of one of the more notable designs in the tombstone pantheon: the faux stump.[4] Lone Fir has a particularly large collection, ten, only seven of which have legible dates beginning in 1891 and continuing to 1912. Not only is a stone tree stump remarkable enough in any cemetery, but the fact that no two are alike is even more astounding. The faux stump was an option, not a requirement for WOW members, so most of their monuments are not naturalistic, but they, certainly, enliven a cemetery. Orders were processed locally, with the home office sending out drawings of how the stumps were to look, but the whims of the carvers resulted in each being different. No one followed the drawings, and often it appears the drawings weren't even consulted. Stott's informative article on the WOW monument program says that the first "tree trunk monuments" were delivered "between February and June of 1893"[5]; in contrast to the earliest death date on a WOW faux stump in Lone Fir of 1891. That monument could, of course, have been erected considerably after the recorded death.

The sixty-seven WOW markers in Lone Fir are joined by some thirteen from Women of Woodcraft covering a diversity of styles; although twenty-eight of the WOW markers and eight of the Women of Woodcraft are variations on the square pillar or stubby obelisk. The WOW monuments are nearly all inscribed with their emblem of a bird flying over a log which props up a maul and from which protrudes an

axe; the whole supported by a semicircular banner carrying the Latin phrase, *dum tactet clamat*: "though silent, he speaks." Sometimes it appears as a metal medallion affixed to the stone. The Women of Woodcraft employ a similar devise.

The year 1904 was the heyday of WOW in Lone Fir. Eleven WOW markers with that date exist in the cemetery, though by ten years later the program was essentially finished. The last WOW date is 1923, nine years after the penultimate. The program, as far as Lone Fir is concerned, lasted primarily twenty-four years.

Another set of "tombstones" from around the same period which also provides visual interest, are the "white bronze" monuments. In one way or another, all white bronze markers originated from the Monumental Bronze Company of Bridgeport, Connecticut, although the finishing work may have been distributed to several other facilities. "In 1881 Bridgeport set up its first subsidiary, in Detroit. After that it established plants in Philadelphia; New Orleans; St. Thomas, Ontario; and the two longest-lasting plants, Western Bronze in Des Moines and American Bronze in Chicago."[6]

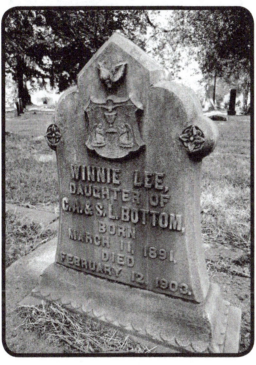

White bronze—which is really zinc[7]—is used in statuary as well as cemetery monuments. Many a town square has been enhanced with a general astride a horse or with a Civil War soldier cast in that familiar dark blue/gray metal. The story of white bronze is of an excellent product getting lost in marketing. After experimenting with and perfecting the product, Monumental Bronze was incorporated in 1879, although the first white bronze markers don't show up in Lone Fir until 1882. The latest date for one is 1905, and their peak hit in 1899.[8] Apparently, they never stumbled upon the idea of having a salesroom where model monuments could be viewed, and their entire business rested on catalog and word-of-mouth in an Avon kind of way; excepting they only had a one-time, single-use product; so in spite of having a product which is holding up extremely well through years of West Coast weathering, there hasn't been a white bronze marker erected in Lone Fir for better than a century.[9]

The company folded in 1939. The president of Monumental Bronze, Ralph Sperry, in the age-old tradition of blaming the government for ones own poor business decisions, lamented, "The constantly increasing tax burden and government restrictions make the business no longer profitable to run."[10] It's a wonder that any businesses have survived at all.

White bronze markers tended to be constructed of molded panels soldered together. Often the name and particulars were molded onto a separate plate which was bolted to the monument. Due to weathering or vandalism, those bolts have occasionally worn through and the panel lost, giving rise to a legend that such markers were used as drop-off exchange points for bootleggers during Prohibition. My own experience with the illegal drug market (market research only, for sure) says that very few people are willing to leave either their product or their money unattended. But it makes for a quaint story. Crystal Lake Cemetery in Salem even incorporates it into their promotional brochure.

If white bronze has a weakness, it's that—aside from its willingness to crack when smashed with a blunt object—it "creeps," which is metallurgical parlance for "slow flow." Zinc is such a soft metal that it "melts" under its own weight much as ice does; and given enough time, any zinc construction would eventually be reduced to a puddle of metal. The larger the construction, the greater the effect. Some statues have had to be cut open and fitted with an interior skeleton to relieve the pressure from gravity.

THE PETRIFIED FOREST

The distribution of monument styles is not uniform throughout the cemetery, reflecting early development patterns. In 2010 and 2011, I conducted an informal survey of the monuments at Lone Fir, looking for ones in five basic categories: Woodmen of the World; white bronze; ones with interesting epitaphs; ones with "cameos," either photoceramics or engravings (excepting the large category of laser-etched, Eastern European tombstones, which require a survey of their own); and ones of interesting design, which includes most of the homemade, as well as others. Admittedly, "interest" is an entirely subjective category. Some tombstones, inevitably, fall into more than one category—an unusual design coupled with a thoughtful epitaph, for example—so that my assignment to categories furthers the arbitrary nature of the project. On the other hand, I tried to be complete in recording the WOW and white bronze monuments and their dates. I was less faithful, but still fairly complete in recording all the photoceramics and portrait etchings, and fairly faithful with homemade monuments.

The northern border of Lone Fir Cemetery is ninety rods long, 1485 feet. Surveyors are fond of rods. The original cemetery extended forty rods east from its northwest corner and forty rods south. The current configuration extends the eastward run another fifty rods and pushes the southern boundary another ten rods beyond its original size. The Macleay Mausoleum—the grandest private mausoleum in the state, bar none—near the "Public Park," more or less backs onto the center of the cemetery. The largest concentration of interesting stones clusters around the mausoleum and the park. There are almost no WOW or white bronze markers in the original ten acres. Combined, there are only nine (of sixty-seven) in the western third of the cemetery.

The MacLeay and Bottler mausoleums are still (2012) awaiting restoration, but a small brick shed behind MacLeay has acquired a new door with wrought-iron support plates in a pineapple plant design. As much as any ornament in the cemetery, this door represents the spirit of Lone Fir: craftsmanship and care.

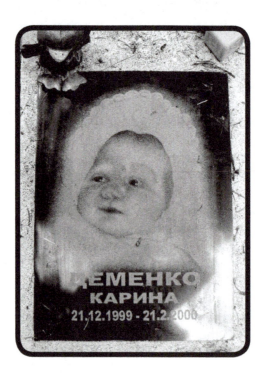

Notes

[1] James Stephens was a wheeler-dealer who engaged in many pursuits after arriving in Oregon, including buying and selling a considerable amount of land. By one account, he at one point sold all his land to join the California gold rush, but came back within a couple years and started all over again. He originally opened a store in Oregon City and eventually ran a ferry there for seventeen years.

[2] D. A. Lund writing under the psuedonym Charles Oluf Olson; "Lone Fir: Silent City of the Dead."

[3] Most of the historical data on the Woodmen of the World comes from Annette Stott's 2003 article, "The Woodmen of the World Monument Program" in *Markers XX*, Greenfield, MA: http://www.archive.org/details/markers20asso.

[4] Not all faux stump markers are WOW; their sister organization, Women of Woodcraft, also sponsored faux stumps; and occasionally non-affiliated faux stumps were erected. It should be mentioned that neither WOW nor Women of Woodcraft actually had (or has) anything to do with woodworking.

[5] Op cit, pg. 6.

[6] "White Bronze Markers," Barbara Rotundo, *Markers FAQ*, "http://www.gravestonestudies.org/faq.htm#White%20Bronze%20Markers."

[7] There is also a jeweler's "white bronze," which is zinc alloyed with copper and tin.

[8] There is a rare white bronze WOW marker from 1903 in Lone Fir.

[9] The Mother Lode of white bronze markers in Oregon is at the Tillamook IOOF Cemetery. It must have nearly fifty white bronze markers, a phenomenal number.

[10] From "The End of an American Company," *Bridgeport, CT Post*, March 8, 1939; online at "http://www.civilwarmonument.org/monumental_bronze.htm."

Stones, Monuments & Markers

The markers are divided into five categories:

Designs
Epitaphs, Unusual Names & Personages
Portraits
Woodmen of the World & Friends
White Bronze

The location number is in the format: "block number.lot number" (e.g.: 25.68). There are a series of maps at the end of the book that begin with an overview of the entire cemetery and then break it down by rows of blocks. You can locate any marker on those maps. That being said, it's not always easy to pinpoint where one is in the cemetery. There can be error in my placement on the map; it's not an exact science. Be patient. If it helps, Stark Street is to the north.

Designs

1.1   Obelisk - exquisite carving, truncated cedar in a circle - *Crawford Dobbins*

1.18   Stephens Memorial - 3/4 life-size - *Eliza and James Stephens*

1.30   Obelisk - "Pioneer's Rest" - *Finice Caruther*

2.16   Punch bowl - *W. H. Frush*

3.21   Flat - hand-engraved script in granite - *Roosevelt Baker*

3.22   Flat - etching of a lighthouse - *Helen Conoly*

3.219 Small upright - engraving of early Oregonian office building - *Thomas Dryer*

4.53   Simple (broken) slab surrounded by four redwoods - *Daniel Wright*

4.68   Three children's gravestones - *Villafuente*

4.80   Stone swallowing tree

4.270 Flat - ying/yang symbol - *Peter Stachelrodt*

5   Firemen's block - There are plans afoot to landscape this area

6.82   Bottler Mausoleum - *George Bottler*

6M.3A Stele- carving of a man's hands above a raging sea; see "Notables" - *Frederic Roeder*

6M.5B Tree swallowing a headstone

7M.210 Handmade bench, "Be still and know that I am"

7M.30 Granite bench with small sarcophagus; see "Notables" - *Helen & Dale Jones*

7M.218 Flat, partly buried stone with metal rose medallion - *Lila Rose*

8.31   Obelisk with AOUW (Ancient Order of United Workmen) symbol - *John Cotter*

8.58   Obelisk - haut relief carving of a face, severely

weathered

motif hinge plates

17.2.G   Stone swallowing tree - *Jane Lucke*

17.3   MacLeay Mausoleum - *MacLeay Family*

17.4.D   Handmade wooden cross - *Lopez*

17.5.C.G   Collapsed vaults, end stones still standing - *A. G. & Cynthia Cunningham*

18.1.H   Two homemade stele; see "Notables" - *George & Martha Otay*

18.208 Upright - handprints on verso, photoceramic; see "Notables" - *Constance Olds*

20.23(A)   Upright - bike riding skeleton; see "Notables" - *Joel Weinstein*

20.30   Natural stone with name scratched into steel "box" affixed to the stone; base for a bronze stature currently in storage - *T. Talbert*

20.39   Upright - black granite, NHRA racing decals and laser cut portrait; see "Notables" - *Shawn Miller*

22.42   Slender column topped with cloth-draped urn. The Murrays sold the original ten acres to Colburn Barrell. *Seldon & Hiantha Murray*

22.6   Commercial statue backing a flat stone bearing the common epitaph: "I have fought the good fight, / I have finished the race, / I have kept the faith." - *Adam Mielnik*

22.16 Granite block - *Wheeler Family*

22.49 Elaborately carved four-sided stone with a cathedral roof capped by a cloth-draped vase - carvings of the American flag and Odd Fellows symbols - *Hill*

25.13 "Adobe" mission-style, curved stone; see "Notables" - *Rosalinda Alfaro*

25.72 Scrabble board - handmade, full-color stele; see "Notables" - *Paul Lind*

25.86 Faux stump - not Woodman of the World - weathered; no name or dates

26.30 Black granite ball inscribed with dragons; see "Notables" - *Minh & Mary Tran*

26.40 Heritage rose garden; see "Notables"

26.202 Granite block slightly taller than broad - *Steven Clay*

27.6 Upright - hand-formed and painted - *Antonia Berezhinskaya*

28.3 Natural stone - whale engraving, epitaph; see "Notables" - *Maxine McCloskey*

30.40 Natural stone - one man, two fish, three trees; see "Notables" - *David Lesman*

34.5 Handmade concrete cross - *Mary Keenan & Lisette Stephens*

34.273 Handmade mosaic cross - *Jesus Morales*

36.10   Small mausoleum - *Mathilde Moran*
36.78   Small upright, race car engraving - *Donald Collins*
36.201   Handmade Orthodox cross - *Aaron Trusty*
36.207   Pair of handmade wooden crosses - *Carlos Chaves*
37.22   Small natural rock - *Warren Black*
37.219(A) Natural rock - *Lindquist Family*
38.16   Small mausoleum - *Burns*
38.20   Handmade and lettered concrete upright - *Maria Black*
38.69(A)   Upright with portraits & epitaph; illustrator - *John & Alta Haelen*
38.292   Handmade upright, palm tree design - *Joan Almason*
39.6   Flush; hand-carved lettering in concrete - *Salvatrice*
39.91   Tapered upright, handmade concrete - *Conrad Kniss*
B.4   Flat - unusual hand-carved clasping hands, flowers - *Carlo Bonando*
C.5   Flat - carving of earth moving equipment - *Clarence Greer*

EPITAPHS, UNUSUAL NAMES & PERSONAGES

1.17   Upright - "My beloved saw mill & logger man" - *Robert Keys*
1.225   Flat - "Fragrance of her life still lives" - *Myrtle May Fee*
2.8   Tall, square pillar - "Crowned Queen Mother Oregon Pioneer 1930" & "Last survivor of Applegate wagon train 1843" - *Anna & John Cullen*
2.14   Pillow - "45th Balloon Co. A.E.F." - *Julius Robinson*
2.25   Short upright - "Pathfinder of Oregon's waters" - *Leonard White*
3.215   Pillow - poem "Folks in heaven don't do a thing…"; see "Notables" - *Golda Miller*
4.270   Flat - yin/yang; "Beloved, courageous, warrior" - *Peter Stachelrodt*
4.47   Obelisk - "Union of brother & sister" - *G. Wilson*
6M.3A.2   Stele, "Gathered in a good old age to the/ assembly of the righteous." - *Alex. Thompson*
7.11   Flat fronting a bench - e. e. cummings poem, "I carry your heart with me (I carry it/ in my heart). I am never without it." - *Ronan Donahue*
7.32   Upright - "Lo, where the silent marble weeps/ A friend, a wife, a mother sleeps:/ A heart within whose

sacred cell / The peaceful virtues loved to dwell." - *J. S. Keller*

8.18   Large slab - long poem by Robinson Jeffers; see "Notables" - *Sara Holzman*

8M.43 Obelisk for *James Hawthorne*

8M.50 Stele for *Asa Lovejoy*

9M.22 Black granite upright - epitaph from Victor Hugo - see "Notables" - *Maureen Rahman*

9M.203   Flat - "A loving lady and loyal wife. / A gravious lady in all ways. / An artist among her flowers / With tender care to every one. / She rests, here, in fond / Remembrance kindly won." - *Ota & Lorelei Pierce*

10.85   Flat - "Just as I am" - *Carolyn Black*

11.7   Flat- "…how we would make the kisses fly." - *Ira Goodell*

11.51   Flat - unusual name - *Cupid Crawford*

11.81   Flat - "May the eye of God be on / this sacred ground," "His spirit smiles from that / bright shore, / And softly whispers, / 'Weep no more'" - *Isabel & Angus MacDonald*

11.82   Flat - unusual name - *Fortunata Cioffi*

11.210   Flat - "I believe I can fly" - *Deborah Bradley*

12.3   Upright with a plaque on the back. "In token of the lasting / gratitude for the sympathy / and gentle kindness of a woman / who, next to his mother, shaped / his mind and character" - *Isabel Belveridge*

12.6 Upright - "He loved Linda," "She loved Bob" - *Robert Lundberg & Linda Toenniessen*

12.211 Upright - "Where there was hate, she sowed love…" - six line poem; see "Notables" - *Phillipa & Richard Harrison*

16.7 Pillow - "Born in the country / Raised in the sticks" - *Elsie Perry*

16.25 Bolster - " 18.1.C Upright with unusual name - *Leaner Gray*

18.6.D Fat obelisk - "Shall I have naught…" - *Fannie Hamshaw*

19.10 Flat - "Just another day in paradise" - etching of sailboat - *Tommie Alexander*

19.19 Upright - "Rather than 'pay it back' - as if it were a loan / We need to 'pay it forward' - / To share the love we've been shown" - *Richard & Ruth Ketchum*

19.231 Epitaph "Play ball"; see "Notables"- Julius Ceasar

20.1 Pillow - "AIDS took our life / But not our love / We won" - *David Benton & Scott Steele*

20.205 Pillow - "Bob carried Dodie's book to [?]" - *D. W. & R. J. Greer*

20.209 Slant - "Strength to survive war / Courage to seek new shores" - *Pluen & Elizabeth Visser*

21.2 Pillow dedicated to Joseph Lane, 1st territorial governor - *Joseph Lane*

22.19   Flat - "From childhood's hour…"; see "Notables"
- *Donald Johnson*

22.50   Pillow - "Keep your face to the sunshine/ and you
cannot see the shadows." - *Wendy Hood*

22.203 Stele - long excerpt from Romeo and Juliet; See
"Notables" - *Jason Hatfield*

22.207 Tall pillow - "Josie, Josie, I can't wait to see you/
I can't wait to be with you/ I can't wait to sit next to
you/ I can't wait to be in heaven with you," "A song/
Your son Jack" - *Josie Cohen*

22.211 Pillow - "Through thick & thin" - *Donna Mason*

28.34   Flat - "Never regret/ Never pretend" - *Michael
Browning*

32.1   Tall square pillar - "She has crossed the mystic
river,/ Her toils and trials are o're,/ Her weary feet, so
need of rest,/ Has reached the shining shore." - *Albert
Harris*

33.21   Flat (behind large upright) "whiter than snow"
- *Essie West*

33.53   Supplemental flush plaque - "Bruce's Group"
Heron Lakes Golf Course - *John Hansen*

34.41   Flush "and baby Violet May" - *Blanche Newman*

35.187 Small flush (next to square pillar) "Waiting" - *Fred*

37.1   Upright: "Some where, some time,/ We'll understand." - *Jess Nudsen*

37.219(B)   Ledger - "My soul is a candle that burned away
the veil,/ Only the glorious duties of light I now have."
St. John of the Cross - *Dorothy Boyd*

38.73   Upright - "At evening time it shall be light" - *John*

& Eleanor Smith

39.33 Flat, unusual name - *Fern Ridge*

39.74 Flat - Confederate soldier - *Melchizedeck Chandler*

D.10 Flat, name - *Fried Egger*

Portraits

7.87 Pillow - photoceramic - *Renalda Mitchell*

10.13 Flat - portrait etching and ones of a locomotive and the Union Pacific logo - *Joseph Allen*

10.58 Flat - "Big Bubba" and bottle of rum and Corona - *James Declue*

10.217 Flat stone etching - *Lillian Branch*

12.70 Flat double etching - modern clothing styles - *James Allen Curtis, Sr. & Jr.*

12.90 Flat - engraving, portrait plus four aces - *Raeco Jones*

13.5 Upright - photoceramic - *Elsa Kahssai*

16.24 Upright - etching of deceased as child and as adult - *Alvin Hicks, Jr.*

16.247 Flat - photoceramic - *Loretha Williams*

17.4.D Flat - photoceramic - *Joan St. Claire*

18.1.D Large portrait etching - *Darrell Glass*

20.23(B) Flat - photoceramic - *Tom, Jr. & Dorothy Moore*

21.26 Slant - photoceramic - *Audrey Price*

22.3 Laser etching on a heart-shaped, black granite upright - *Sara Sanchez*

22.230 Small upright - "Our beloved Spoofer" - photoceramic; fronted by a heart-shaped stone with a photoceramic of the Spoofer's missus "Fantastic" - *Russell & Dorothy Royse*

22.203 Upright - laser portrait on black granite - *Tan Nguyen*

22.209 Flat - etched portrait - *Helen Ports*

24.243 Small upright - photoceramic - *Ora Martin*

25.80 Upright - photoceramic - "She was the brightest light in our lives" - *Doris Johnson*

30.28 Flat - etching with epitaph: "You may not have wings/ Yet you are always there/ You may not have a halo/ Yet you surround us with love"; "If there are angels on earth/ For kind things people do? I'm sure as heaven above/ That one was you" - *Mary Spain*

36.23 Upright double cameo, front/back; flanked by two laser portraits; see "Notables" - *Michael Parker*

36.212   Matched pair of pillows; engraved portraits - *Mary & Walter Lewis*

38.213   Flush photceramic; guitar etching - *Norman Mc-Cloud*

C.8   Flat photoceramic - *Darryl English*

Woodmen of the World & Friends

3.25   Upright, no date - *Thomas Strowbridge*

6.49   Upright 1914 - *Jacob Hohbach*

8.76   Upright 1913 - *Thomas Dean*

11.43   Small Upright 1896 - *Albert Brown*

16.43   Upright - red granite 1909 - *John Everest*

17.2.H   Square pillar, faded engraving, no date - *Joseph Floyd*

18.1.E An unusual combination of white bronze and Woodman of the World - *William Moreland*

18.1.F One of a set of 5 raised pillows in an unusual book design - *Strowbridge & Muellerhaupt*

18.4.G   Obelisk 1923 - *William & Ella Ostrander*

19.28   Woman of Woodcraft - square pillar 1910 - *Ottilie Jacks*

19.47   Woman of Woodcraft - raised bolster 1913 - *Agnes Liddle*

21.18   Woman of Woodcraft - upright 1909 - *Deliah Sargent*

21.45   Upright - log top 1905 - *Anton Matschek*

22.28   Upright 1914 - *Alexander Fink*

25.18   Square pillar 1901 - *Sidney Spreadborough*

25.68   Square pillar, worn, no date

26.50   Short upright surmounted by a bolster 1905 - *James Graham*

27.3   Neighbors of Woodcraft - upright 1930 - *Christene Berg*

28.38   Woman of Woodcraft - square pillar 1908 - *Mary Beck*

28.41   Square pillar 1903 - *Otto Panck*

28.207 Large square pillar 1898 - *William Wood*

28.209 Large upright 1909 - *William Munro*

29.7   Faux stump 1891 - *J. A. Tell*

29.41   Square pillar 1907 - *Steve Jemmos*

29.45   Square pillar 1907 - *Otto Brandes*

29.47S Woman of Woodcraft, small obelisk 1907 - *Matilda Palmer*

30.41   Faux stump - no date - *N. Martin Hansen*

30.45   Small square pillar 1906 - *Almond Holden*

30.57   Flat 1907 - *Michael McGloin*

31.23   Square pillar 1897 - *Phillip Young*

31.68   Squat square pillar 1901 - *John Boy*

31.204 Square pillar 1900 - *Marcus Duntley*

31.205 Upright 1920 - *Colby Smith*

31.233 Faux stump 1912 - *John Hammond*

32.20   Square pillar - "Like the dove in the ark, / Thou hast flown to thy rest, / From the wild sea of strife, / To the home of the blessed." 1896 - *Peter Calsing*

32.62   Square pillar 1904 - *Thad Fisher*

33.70   Flat, sunk in the ground 1904 - *David White*

34.7(B)   Neighbors of Woodcraft, flush - *Susan Schacht*

34.12   Woman of Woodcraft, square pillar, - *Maria Oelsner*

34.24　Upright 1907 - *Ivan & Laura Guthrie*
34.61　Faux stump 1901 - *Thomas Burton*
34.68　Faux stump 1897 - *Gilbert Anderson*
34.70　Upright 1902 - *Wesley Porth*
34.84　Square pillar 1900 - *James Hair*

34.98　Faux stump 1907 - *Chas. Wise*
34.106　Large square column 1890 - *Charles Hoyt*
34.107　Faux stump, no date - *Aksel Johnson*
34.220　Woman of Woodcraft upright 1916 - *Emma Conser*
35.17　Square pillar 1905 - *Ralph Warner*
35.32　Square pillar - *Thomas Davoren*
35.76　Faux stump, no date - *Elmer White*
35.92　Faux stump 1904 - *Herman Norby*
35.101　Square pillar 1904 - *Charles Fransen*
35.121(A)　Square pillar 1904 - *Robert Nordstrom*
35.121(B)　Woman of Woodcraft, upright 1907 - *Frederica MacDonald*
35.130　Upright 1914 - *Andrew Horberg*
35.136　Faux stump 1904 - *August Koch*
36.36　Small double 1899, 1903 - *Ross & Ruth Field*
36.48　Small upright 1906 - *R. E. Rasmussen*
36.56　Upright, log top 1903 - *Ferdinand Drews*
36.69　Upright 1906 - *Harry Scott*
37.5(A)　Square pillar 1902 - *Charles Stahl*
37.5(B)　Half-bolster 1908 - *Benj. Stahl*
37.23 - Woman of Woodcraft, square pillar 1902 - *Mary Peterson*
37.29　Square pillar 1901 - *George Ledyard*
37.45　Upright 1919 - *John Richen*
37.59　Neighbors of Woodcraft, pillow 1934 - *Johan & Belle Jorgensen*
37.85　Neighbors of Woodcraft, pillow 1929 - *Mina Bart-*

man

38.12 Upright 1905 - *G. Edward Carlson*

38.19 Square pillar 1902 - *Winfield & Moak*

38.30 Square pillar 1901 - *Edward Inglenrock*

38.69(B) Square pillar; chess castle 1902 - *John Haelen*

38.86 Square pillar 1902 - *George Benson*

38.88 Woman of Woodcraft, square pillar 1902 - *Laura McQuaid*

38.207 Unusual pillow header for a ledger 1901 - *John Leasure*

39.3 Square pillar 1902 - *George Smith*

39.12 Square pillar - *E. Watson*

39.18 Square pillar 1904 - *Thomas Anderson*

39.42 Woman of Woodcraft, square pillar 1903 - *Loui Helling*

39.53 Ledger, French 1902 - *Paul Kisslow*

39.62 Upright 1912 - *George Kurtz*

39.92 Upright 1904 - *Antone Pfeifer*

39.154 Square pillar 1906 - *Frederick Jensen*

D.1 Square pillar 1897 - *John Christen*

D.7 Stubby obelisk 1899 - *Andrew Ruhndorf*

D.11 Square pillar 1901 - *William Sprague*

E.5 Woman of Woodcraft, Square pillar 1904 - *Mary Ikeman*

E.6 Woman of Woodcraft, Stubby obelisk 1904 - *Elizabeth Erenhart*

White bronze

6.65 Obelisk - mother & father headers 1905 - *Anna Winters*

8M.52 Trio of markers 1882, 1886, 1904

9.43 Short obelisk 1888, 1903 - *Taylor/Mutsoker*

10.81 Double, plus a single upright 1899, 1895 - *Minnie & Versy Darling*

11.60 Small upright 1882 - *Jose Stuart*

11.79 Small flat plate sunk in concrete 1899 - *Peter Schwabauer*

13.25 Two square uprights 1887, 1900 - *William & Minerva Odell*

18.6F Double, large & small 1899 - *Robert Hunter*

20.15 Large upright and small slant 1905, 1885 - *Mary & Charles Joslyn*

21.5 Small upright 1899 - *Rachel Perry*

21.23 Obelisk 1889 - *Mary Johnson*

24.27 Slender obelisk with two foot "stones" 1904 - *Eliza Richardson*

26.12 Square pillar 1890 - *Eugene Johnson*

28.40 Obelisk 1893 - *Lorenz Bohnert*

29.20 Small upright 1900 - *Amelia Koppe*

30.9 Small square pillar 1901 - *W. M. Scott*

30.68S Small upright 1902 - *Martha Rose*

31.53 Upright - retrieve date - *Edgar Rofeno*

31.67 Small upright 1901 - *Annie Fuchs*

33.8 Small flush, no date "Baby" - *Jonathan Bessie*

33.26 Slant 1895 - *John Ray*

34.1 Obelisk 1896 - *P. W. Ross*

34.7(A) Upright 1899 - *L. D. Miller*

34.16 Peaked pillow 1900, 1901 - *George & Mary Krueger*

34.79 Square pillar 1899 - *Helen Freed*

38.10 Upright 1901 - *Rosanna Simpson*

38.82 Small upright - *Winnie Bottom*

Soldier's Monument

THE G.A.R. (GRAND ARMY OF THE REPUBLIC) was instrumental nationally in erecting countless statues commemorating the Civil War. They've shared this statue with the veterans of the Spanish American and Indian Wars, but it was the G.A.R. that steamrolled the project. They went so far as to establish entire cemeteries in sometimes curious locations; besides Portland (there's one within Greenwood Hills Cemetery above River View Cemetery), there are G.A.R. cemeteries in Newberg and Bandon. This statue was dedicated in 1903 at a cost of $4150. Part of the funds was raised by enacting a "sham battle" between veterans of the Spanish-American and Indian Wars and members of the National Guard, at a nearby baseball diamond. Spectators watched the action which commenced with participants eating a large mess of beans. *The Oregonian* (May 30, 1903) reported, "Suddenly the wicked Filipinos lurking in the darkness of the outer edges of the grounds fired upon the pickets, who returned the same with spirit. The hospital corps rushed off with stretchers and brought in the wounded, while the vets continued to enjoy the campfire sports with great disregard of the villainous enemy."

The Lone Fir

THE ARBORETUM

WHEN *NATIONAL GEOGRAPHIC* CHOSE LONE FIR as one of the "top ten cemeteries to visit" in the world, it did so partly because it's "one of the few cemeteries that allows the planting of a tree or garden to commemorate the dearly departed."[1] This is in contrast to lawn cemeteries where you're not encouraged to commemorate the dead, or with modern "green" cemeteries where one is planted in the forest and located by GPS. They don't encourage plastic flowers or Teddy Bears there, either.

When Lone Fir acquired its name in 1866, it was named appropriately: there was but one tree on the property. That fir still stands and is marked by a commemorative plaque. It has since been joined by some six hundred other trees and bushes, twenty per acre. And that's not counting the flower gardens adorning many of the burials, especially those modern ones of Eastern European immigrants.

Today, a minimum of seventy-one species of trees shelter the cemetery. More than a hundred of the trees are cedars of one sort or another and better than eighty are firs and more than sixty are maples. The perennial favorite and vigorous spreader, holly, corrals some fifty-five specimens, one of which is variegated. Other species of note include elm, birch, chestnut, buckeye, horsechestnut, oak, and nine sequoia. These are joined by a smattering of dogwood, hemlock, yew, and linden, as well as others. Interestingly enough, there are only seven rhododendrons in the cemetery and numerous species are represented by only a few specimens, such as willow, locust, quince, copper beech, hawthorn, eucalyptus, ginkgo, and cherry.

For many decades there was an elm that finally succumbed to old age, which was thought to be a scion of the Washington elm in Boston Commons where George took command of the revolutionary army; but there was never any proof that Barrel didn't simply drag an elm up from San Francisco with him. There were scions of the Washington elm spread across the nation, but none in Oregon, as far as we know.

As an arboretum, Lone Fir lacks the diversity and planning that an official arboretum might contain, simply because all the trees were planted by separate individuals without regard to what else the cemetery already contained. Probably, if anyone was watching over the place, the forest would never have been allowed to grow so rampant; but, despite occasional bursts of preservation and landscaping, until Metro assumed control of the pioneer cemeteries, benign neglect was the best description to apply to the property. Even Metro, when they first took over the cemeteries, tried to dump them onto the market; but, needless-to-say, no one wanted to buy fourteen pioneer cemeteries on the West Coast. To Metro's credit, once they realized they couldn't divest themselves of the cemeteries, they took their maintenance seriously and the cemeteries are enjoying their best days yet. Nonetheless, by the time Metro took over, the trees were already grown, the arboretum was in place. Their job has been to keep it in check.

The lesson here is that those trees helped Lone Fir to become an international celebrity. For the cognoscenti, there will forever be debate as to whether or not Lone Fir is the best cemetery in the county, much less the entire state. Mountain View Corbett, Jacksonville, Agency at Warm Springs, and the estimable Camp Polk Cemetery all have their partisans; but given Lone Fir's location, diversity, upkeep, and spirit of independence—not to mention all those trees—it's understandable that the casual visitor to the state thinks this is all we have. Well, it may be among the best in the world, but it's also among the best in the state. We are blessed.

---

[1] http://travel.nationalgeographic.com/travel/top-10/cemeteries/#page=2

A recent arboreal survey done on Metro's bequest turned up the following list of species, plus a few trees which were indeterminate:

ailanthus	European white birch
American elm	fir
arborvitae	flowering cherry
ash	ginkgo
basswood	golden cedar
beech	grand fir
big leaf maple	great silver fir
bing cherry	hawthorn
birch	hemlock
blue spruce	holly
buckeye	honey locust
cedar	horsechestnut
chamaecyparis	incense cedar
cherry	Japanese pine
chestnut	Kwanzan cherry
copper beech	laceleaf Japanese maple
cutleaf birch	lilac
cypress	linden
cypress shrub	locust
deodar cedar	magnolia
dogwood	maple
Douglas fir	mountain ash
elm	Norway maple
eucalyptus	oak

Oregon oak
pin oak
pine
pink dogwood
Port Orford cedar
quince apple
red leaf maple
red oak
rhododendron
sequoia
southern magnolia

spruce
sweet gum
sycamore
tulip tree
weeping ash
weeping cherry
western hemlock
western red cedar
willow
yew
Young's weeping birch

Bottler Mausoleum

THE SMALL GEORGE F. BOTTLER MAUSOLEUM is in serious need of repair—trees grow through the roof—and is on the cemetery's short-list. The appropriately named Bottler opened Portland's second brewery, City Brewery, selling out to Henry Weinhard in 1864. It's hoped that eventually the city's current crop of craft brewers will see to a full restoration of the building erected in 1865 by George's brother, a Portland fireman. One assumes it was proceeds from the sale to Weinhard which financed construction.

LAST WORDS
A GLOSSARY OF BURIAL TERMS

BIER

A platform on which a corpse or a coffin containing a corpse is placed prior to burial, or a coffin along with its stand.

Coming via Old English from similar words (e.g. beere*) having the sense of "to carry," witness such words as "bear," as in to bear children, or "barrow," as in wheel barrow.*

BLACK GLASS

An 8x10 rectangle of black glass into which the deceased's name and statistics were etched and subsequently embedded in stone or concrete, popular in the late 1930s and early 40s; manufactured by Memorial Arts in Portland.

> Born in the country..
> Raised in the sticks
> -Elsie Perry

"Black," like its antonym "white," is essentially unchanged in meaning through time. "Glass" likewise has retained an ancient meaning, originally from a presumed Indo-european root ghel-, *"to shine or glitter, especially with a green or yellow cast.*

CASKET

Container in which a corpse is buried or cremated.

Of uncertain origin, it predates "cask" which precludes it being a diminutive of said word.

CATACOMB

A cave, grotto, or large subterranean space used as a burial ground, commonly in the plural.

Borrowed from Latin via Italian. The Latin catacumbae *first designated a set of underground tombs between the second and third milestones of the Appian Way. Before that, its origins are in dispute.*

CATAFALQUE

The stand upon which a coffin rests during viewing or the funeral service. The Catholics also use it as a pall-covered faux-casket used in a requiem mass after the burial.

Taken from the Italian, meaning "scaffold," where the trail gets obscure; but it looks related to the French word for scaffold, échafaut.

CEMETERY

A place for burying the dead; a graveyard. The *Catholic Encyclopedia* says this about "cemetery": "The word *coemeterium* or *cimiterium* (in Gr. *koimeterion*) may be said in early literature to be used exclusively of the burial places of Jews and Christians."

> Gathered in a good old age to the
> assembly of the righteous.
> -Alex. Thompson

Slowly twisted to us from the Latin and French and ultimately the Greek koiman, *"to put to sleep," itself from an Indo-European root with the senses of "to lie; bed, couch; dear, beloved," itself an interesting comment on associations. Other words with the same root include "to hide" and "city."*

CENOTAPH

An empty tomb or a monument erected in honor of a person buried elsewhere.

From the Greek kenos, *"empty," and* taphos, *"tomb." (Keno players take note.)*

CERECLOTH

Cloth coated with wax or gummy matter and formerly used for wrapping dead bodies.

A mongrel word formed by joining the Latin word for wax, cera, *to the English word "cloth."*

CEREMENT

Synonymous with "cerecloth."

From the Latin cera, *"wax," plus the suffix "-ment."*

CHARNEL HOUSE

A building, room, or vault in which the bones or bodies of the dead are placed. Also used without the "house" and as an adjective.

The first syllable "char-" comes down from the Latin through French meaning "flesh." It's the same "char" that appears in "charcuterie," an establishment selling cooked meats, or referring to the contents of such a shop.

> He loved Linda
> She loved Bob
> ~Robert Lundberg & Linda Toennissen

CINERARIUM

A place for maintaining the ashes of a cremated body.

Things having to do with cremation are cinerary, in particular cinerary urns, in which the Romans kept their dead. From the Latin word cinis, *"ashes," whence "incinerate," etc.; which is probably why "columbarium" is preferred for the same thing, the association being with doves instead of fire.*

CLOSE

Gravediggers' cant referring to sealing a grave and backfilling with dirt.

"Close," has retained its meaning and related forms since Latin (via French), where it derives from clausus, *itself the past participle of* claudere, *"to close, enclose, put an end to." It ultimately issues from a Proto-Indo-European root, as well: *klau-, "crooked or forked branch used as a bolt."*

COFFIN

A container in which a corpse is buried or cremated; synonymous with "casket."

Middle English borrowed this French word for "basket." The French borrowed it from the Latins who in turn borrowed it from the Greeks.

COLUMBARIUM

A wall of niches which contain urns or boxes of ashes of the dead; also one of the niches in such a wall.

The Latin word for "dove" is columba. *In much of the Mediter-*
ranean world, dovecotes are built as walls or towers of niches in
which the doves build their nests and from which the farmers can
harvest the eggs and birds. Columbaria look like dovecotes. The
wild columbine looks like five doves facing each other in a circle.
Don't forget Christopher Columbus.

CORONACH
A lamentation for the dead.

With several alternative spellings, from the Gaelic for "a crying."

My soul is a candle that burned away the veil,
Only the glorious duties of light I now have."
St. John of the Cross
-Dorothy Boyd

CREMAINS
A portmanteau word carrying the meaning of "cremated
remains."

For the source of "cremated," see "crematorium" below. "Re-
mains" is ultimately from Latin manere, *"to stay," and the prefix*
"re-," which can have the meaning of "back"; hence, "to remain"
equals "to stay back."

CREMATORIUM
Either the furnace for burning corpses or the building in
which such a furnace is contained.

From the Germanic branch of the Indo-European root ker-, *"heat,*
fire," the source of such diverse words as "hearth, carbon, carbun-
cle, charcoal," and, of course, "cremate."

CRYPT
Underground vault or chamber, especially one beneath a
church that is used as a burial place.

From the Greek via Latin, coming from the Greek word kruptein,
"to hide."

DIRGE
A mournful funeral hymn. A complicated explanation for a
simple history.

It came from the Latin for "to direct," and was part of a call and response routine in the Catholic Office of the Dead, *i.e. their service for the dead. Because of its location as the first word in this mournful response, it eventually became shorthand for the entire service and acquired the meaning of the whole and subsequently took on the independent sense of a hymn to the dead.*

DOLMEN

An ancient Celtic structure most often regarded as a burial chamber, consisting of two upright stones plus a horizontal capstone. Synonymous with "cromlech."

Different sources give different origins for "dolmen," though all point to a Celtic origin. The second syllable, "men," comes from the Celtic word for "stone," men, *which is also encountered in "menhir," upright stones found abundantly singly or in groups in Brittany and Cornwall, in particular.*

> I carry your heart with me (I carry it in my heart). I am never without it.
> [e. e. cummings]
> ~Ronan Donahue

ELEGY

A melancholy song or poem composed in remembrance of the dead.

Essentially unchanged from the Greek in meaning and not too changed in spelling, elegos, *a mournful song.*

EMBALM

The process of preserving a dead body by means of circulating preservatives and antiseptics through the veins and arteries.

Goes back to the Semitic word for "balsam," the plant, whose name is essentially the same as the word "balm"; balsam being a prime ingredient in the process from a very early date. We got it from Old French which brought it from Latin.

EPITAPH

An epitaph can be either the inscription on or at a grave or tomb or a brief writing mimicking a real epitaph.

From the Greek through Latin and French; epi- *meaning "at, upon," while* taphos *means "tomb." Cf. cenotaph.*

ESCHATOLOGY

Eschatology has two senses: one is as a collection of beliefs surrounding death and the end of days; the other is the study of such beliefs. In Christian theology, it's the study of death, judgment, heaven, and hell.

From the Greek eskhatos, "last," plus the common suffix "-logy," which issues from the Greek "to speak," most specifically about a given subject.

EXCARNATION

Sky burial: the removal of flesh from corpses by vultures and other birds.

> AIDS took our life
> But not our love
> We won
> -David Benton & Scott Steele

From the Latin ex-, "from"; and carnis, "flesh." "Excarnation" has broader meanings than "sky burial," and includes any stripping of the flesh from the bones.

GRAVE

"Grave" has three senses relating to death. There is the hole into which the body is interred; which extends to the general place of burial; and, finally, it is allegorical for death itself.

From the Germanic for "trench" or "grave" through various forms of English meaning "to dig, scratch, or engrave." You might think of gravlax, which is salmon that has been buried for a period of time.

HEARSE

Originally the hearse was a harrow-shaped structure for holding candles over a coffin and still retains that meaning, but its more current usage is as the vehicle used for transportation of the casket.

From the Latin word for "harrow," which itself, probably, came from the Oscan word for "wolf," on account of the harrow's resemblance to wolf's teeth.

HYPOGEUM

An ancient subterranean burial chamber, such as a catacomb, usually used by one family or a particular group.

From the Greek word meaning "underground."

LAMENT

As a noun or either a transitive or intransitive verb, it expresses deep grief or mourning.

Another word drifting down through the ages essentially unchanged in form or content. Ultimately from the Latin lamentum, *with the same meaning.*

> Some where, some time,
> We'll understand.
> -Jess Nudsen

LEDGER

Or ledger stone. Stone slab covering most or all of a grave, often with extensive writing.

From the earlier "legger," "book"; probably from a sense of "to lay." "Ledger" is also used in the building trades to denote a particular element of scaffolding support.

LOCULUS

More or less synonymous with "niche," excepting that loculi tend to be reserved for entire remains, whereas niches are reserved for cremated remains.

From the Latin for "little place," loculus, *the diminuative of the Latin* locus, *"place."*

MONOLITH

Any tall, narrow marker such as a column or obelisk made from a single stone.

A combinatorial word from the Greek mónos, *"alone"; and* lithos, *"stone."*

MORGUE

A place where the bodies of the dead are maintained that they may be identified or claimed; a deadhouse.

Named after a building in Paris, La Morgue, *which had the same purpose as the English morgue. Supposition has it that its name came from the word "morgue," meaning a "haughty or arrogant manner," which somehow got transformed into "solemnity"; but there is no direct evidence for such.*

MORTUARY

In current usage it means either a burial place for the dead or a place where the dead can be visited before burial.

Webster's equates "mortuary" with "morgue," but "morgue" has more the sense of "governmental structure," whereas "mortuary" has more the sense of a "private burial home or viewing residence." At one time, a mortuary was a gift given to the minister of the parish of the dead person, ostensibly, to cover any arrears in tithing the dead may have occurred. The panoply of "mort-" words stem from the Latin word for "dead," mortuus. *Besides the obvious, other "mort-" words include "nightmare, morsel, morbid, mortgage, and ambrosia."*

MOS TEUTONICUS

Latin for "German method." The practice during the Crusades of stripping the flesh from the bones of the deceased and transporting them elsewhere, most specifically, back home.

> It is sown in weakness
> It is raised in power
> -John Edgerton

Mos is, as said, Latin for "method." The Teutones *were a Germanic tribe, the name of whom the Romans applied to all Germans.* Teutones, *in turn, comes from a proto-Indo-European word* *teuta *meaning "people." It was common for Europeans to expand the name of a single tribe to cover all Germans; confer French* Alleman *or Scandinavian* Tysk.

NECROPOLIS

Literally, a city of the dead. A cemetery, especially a large and elaborate one belonging to an ancient city.

From a Greek word, the components of which are nekro, *"corpse," and* polis *"city."*

NICHE

A hollowed space in a wall made especially (in this connotation) for placing of urns containing cremated remains.

There are two competing theories as to the origin of "niche." No one argues that we borrowed it from the French, but there's a question of whence the French got it. One school says it's a corruption of the Old Italian word nicchio, *"seashell"; but a better argument is that it's derived from the Latin for "nest,"* nidus, *the argument that* **Petit Robert** *makes. Ultimately, it comes from the Indo-European root* sed-, *from which a whole host of words, including "sit, saddle, settle, sewer, assess, posses, preside, supersede, cathedral, chair, ephedrine, tetrahedron, soil, sedate, banshee," and "soot," derive.*

OBELISK

A tapering, four-sided stone pillar, usually monolithic and capped with a pyramidal apex. In cemeteries, a fashionable imitation of Egyptian custom.

> Keep your face to the sunshine
> and you cannot see the
> shadows
> -Wendy Hood

From the Greek obelískos, *"small spit," derived from* obel(ós), *"spit, pointed pillar" plus the diminutive suffix* -iskos.

OPEN

In gravediggers' cant, it refers to digging a grave: one opens a grave.

"Open" has kept its form, more or less, and its meaning for a long time. Ultimately, it's from the Proto-Indo-European *upo, *"up from under, over," and is related to "up."*

PALL

For the most part, it means an often velvet cloth draped over a coffin, bier, or tomb, but occasionally it refers to the coffin as it's being carried to the grave.

Old English pæll, *"cloak, covering" from the Latin* pallium *meaning the same.*

PILLOW

A (more-or-less) one-foot by two-foot, raised flat marker, so named for its resemblance to the household item.

Ultimately from the Latin pulvinus, *"cushion."*

PYRE

A pile of combustibles for burning a corpse as a funeral rite.

The same word as "fire" only spelled slightly differently, but from the same Indo-European root paw, *"fire."*

REQUIEM

A mass, musical composition, hymn, or service for the dead.

A case of the first word of a long speech coming to represent the entire speech. In this case, the first word of the Catholic mass for the dead is the Latin requis, *"rest," from whence the entire mass or, subsequently, musical composition. The ultimate Indo-European root* kweie, *"quiet," has given rise to many English words, among which "quiet, quite, quit, acquit, coy, whilom," and "while."*

SARCOPHAGUS

Above-ground stone coffin often inscribed or decorated with sculpture.

> At evening time it shall be light
> – John & Eleanor Smith

Ultimately, from the Greek sarx, *"flesh," and* phagein, *"to eat," referring to the supposed properties of limestone when a corpse is placed in it. Originally* sarkophagos, *"flesh-eating," was preceded by* lithos, *"stone," but over time* lithos *got dropped and any stone coffin became a sarcophagus.*

SEPULCHER

A burial vault or receptacle for the dead.

Winding down from Old French which took it from the past participle of the Latin verb sepelre, *"to bury the dead."*

SEXTON

An under-officer of a church who is a Jack-of-All-Trades for the place, including keeping the priest happy, maintaining vestments, ringing bells, being the janitor, digging the graves, and maintaining the graveyard.

Coming to us from Anglo-Latin, it's a synonym for "sacristan," both of which derive from the latin word for "sacred," sacer; *whence, of course, "sacred" itself.*

SHROUD

A cloth used to wrap a body for burial; a winding sheet.

From an Anglo-Saxon word, scrud, *"garment, cloth," it also survives in English as "shred."*

SPOILS

The excess dirt left after an excavation, in this case a grave.

From the Middle English spoilen, *"to plunder"; ultimately from the Latin* spolium, *"booty."*

STELE

An upright slab or pillar carrying an inscription or sculpted design, serving as a marker or commemorative tablet. In architecture it is often incorporated into the facade design of a building.

> whiter than snow
> ~Essie West

From the Greek with the same spelling and meaning; ultimately from the Indo-European *sta- *"to stand, set down, make or be firm." From whence, among others, the suffix "-stan," as in "Pakistan"; "-stan" being the place where one stands.*

THRENODY

A poem or song of mourning.

From the Greek thrnos, *"lament," and* aoid, *"song."*

TOMB

Various senses of being a place for the dead or a monument commemorating them.

From the Greek through Lower Latin through French to English it's been spelled similarly and meant the same. Perhaps related to the Latin tumulus, *"mound."*

URN

A container into which cremated remains are placed, usually made of metal, wood or stone.

Via the Latin urna *of the same meaning.*

VAULT

A burial chamber underground or partly so, including in meaning the outside metal or concrete casket container, as well.

In a bit of allusion, the Indo-European word for "to roll," wel-,
obtained the sense of arching, as in during a roll, and then into a
thing which has an arch; in this case the arch over the tomb (could
have been over the bank). Some other words out of the wel- include, "waltz, willow, wallow, revolve, valley, volume, evolve,
vulva, covering," and "womb."

WAKE
A watch kept over the deceased, possibly lasting the entire
night preceding the funeral.

One has to be awake to keep watch at a wake, all of those words
coming from the Indo-European weg-, "strong, lively." As well as
"vigilante, reveille," and "velocity."

WINDING-SHEET (-CLOTH)
A sheet for wrapping a corpse; a shroud.

From the sense of winding a cloth around the body.

THE MAPS

LET'S BE REALISTIC: there's no easy way to navigate around the cemetery. In theory it's laid out in neat rows of lots, but actually finding those neat rows can be a trial. Few of the markers have any indication of their block or lot numbers. Once you find neighboring numbers, it's a by-guess-and-by-gosh affair of deciding where you actually are. On the following charts, the small gray circles represent trees and are an aid in locating graves.

The following maps, graciously provided by Metro, are, perhaps, not the best solution, but it's the one we've got. The first map shows the entire cemetery and you can orient yourself on the sectional maps by using this master. Below is the key to the symbols. Their locations correspond to the numbers on the Markers list. The master map is then sliced into seven north/south columns, which, except for the first column, are displayed in double-page spreads, top to bottom, left to right. The first column is displayed on a single page opposite the master map.

KEY

■ design
◆ epitaphs & names
▲ portraits
● Woodmen Of the World
✳ white bronze

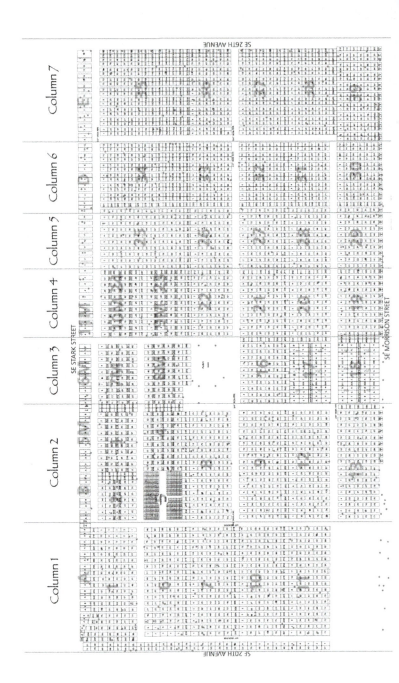

SE 26TH AVENUE

Column 7 | Column 6 | Column 5 | Column 4 | Column 3 | Column 2 | Column 1

SE STARK STREET

SE MORRISON STREET

SE 20TH AVENUE

Maps courtesy of Metro.

METRO

295	A	1	B	A	2	B	A	3	B	A	4	B	A	5	B	A	6	B	A	7	B	A	8	B	A	9	B	10A
71	31	296	294																									
70	30	297	94	93	292	291	270	265	260	255	250	245	240	235	230	225◆	220	215	210	205
69	29	290	90	85	80	75	70	65	60	55	50	45	40	35	30■	25	20	15	10	5
68	28	289	89	84	79	74	69	64	59	54	49	44	39	34	29	24	19	14	9	4
67	27	288	88	83	78	73	68	63	58	53	48	43	38	33	28	23	18■	13	8	3
66	26	287	87	82	77	72	67	62	57	52	47	42	37	32	27	22	17◆	12	7	2
65	25	286	85	81	76	71	66	61	56	51	46	41	36	31	26	21	16	11	6	1■
64	24																			
63	23	1	6	11	16	21	26	31	36	41	46	51	56	61	66	71	76	81	86
62	22	2	7	12	17	22	27	32	37	42	47	52	57	62	67	72	77	82■	87
61	21	3	8	13	18	23	28	33	38	43	48	53	58	63	68	73	78	83	88
60	20	4	9	14	19	24	29	34	39	44	49●	54	59	64	69	74	79	84	89
59	19	5	10	15	20	25	30	35	40	45	50	55	60	65✱	70	75	80	85	90
58	18	201	202	203	204	205	206	207	208	209	210	211	212	213	214	215	216	217	218
57	17	1	2	3	4	5	6	7	8	9	10	11◆	12	13	14	15	16	17	18
56	16	36	35	34	33	32◆	31	30	29	28	27	26	25	24	23	22	21	20	19
55	15	37	38	39	40	41	42	43	44	45	46	47	48	49	50	51	52	53	54
54	14	72	71	70	69	68	67	66	65	64	63	62	61	60	59	58	57	56	55
53	13	73	74	75	76	77	78	79	80	81	82	83	84	85	86	87▲	88	89	90
52	12	201	202	203	204	205	206	207	208	209	210	211	212▲	213	214	215	216	217▲	218■
51	11	1	2	3	4	5	6	7	8	9	10	11	12	13▲	14	15	16	17	18
50	10	36	35	34	33	32	31	30	29	28	27	26	25	24	23	22	21	20	19
49	9	37	38	39	40	41	42	43	44	45	46	47	48	49	50	51	52	53	54
48	8	72	71	70	69	68	67	66	65	64	63	62	61	60	59	58▲	57	56	55
47	7	73	74	75	76	77	78	79	80	81	82	83	84	85◆	86	87	88	89	90
46	6	201	202	203	204	205	206	207	208	209	210◆	211	212	213	214	215	216	217	218
45	5	1	2	3■	4	5	6	7	8	9	10	11	12	13	14	15	16	17	18
44	4	36	35	34	33	32	31	30	29	28	27	26	25	24	23	22	21	20	19
43	3	37	38	39	40	41	42	43	44	45	46	47	48	49	50	51◆	52	53	54
42	2	72	71	70	69	68	67	66	65	64	63	62✱	61	60	59	58	57	56	55
41	1	73	74	75	76	77	78	79✱	80	81◆	82◆	83	84	85	86	87	88	89	90

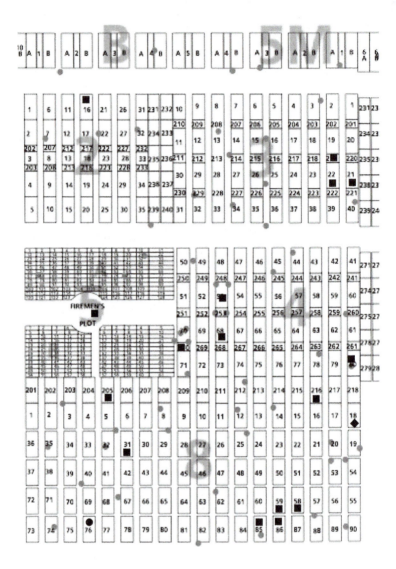

Column 2

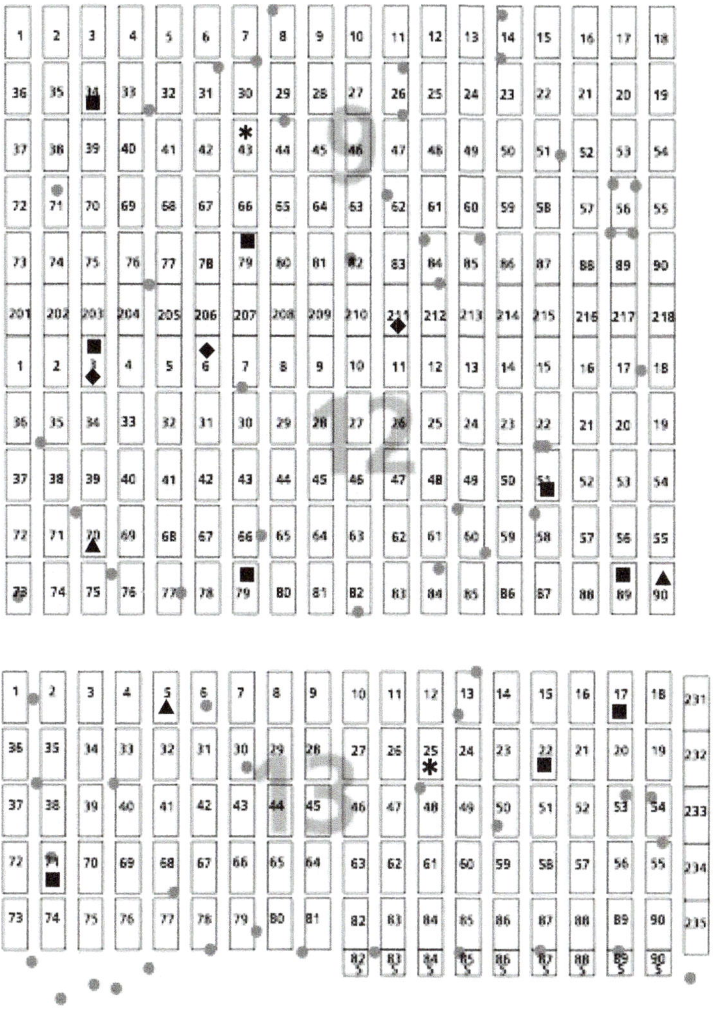
9
1 2 3 4 5 6 7 8 9 10 11 12 13 14 15 16 17 18
36 35 34 33 32 31 30 29 28 27 26 25 24 23 22 21 20 19
37 38 39 40 41 42 43 44 45 46 47 48 49 50 51 52 53 54
72 71 70 69 68 67 66 65 64 63 62 61 60 59 58 57 56 55
73 74 75 76 77 78 79 80 81 82 83 84 85 86 87 88 89 90
201 202 203 204 205 206 207 208 209 210 211 212 213 214 215 216 217 218
12
1 2 3 4 5 6 7 8 9 10 11 12 13 14 15 16 17 18
36 35 34 33 32 31 30 29 28 27 26 25 24 23 22 21 20 19
37 38 39 40 41 42 43 44 45 46 47 48 49 50 51 52 53 54
72 71 70 69 68 67 66 65 64 63 62 61 60 59 58 57 56 55
73 74 75 76 77 78 79 80 81 82 83 84 85 86 87 88 89 90
13
1 2 3 4 5 6 7 8 9 10 11 12 13 14 15 16 17 18 231
36 35 34 33 32 31 30 29 28 27 26 25 24 23 22 21 20 19 232
37 38 39 40 41 42 43 44 45 46 47 48 49 50 51 52 53 54 233
72 71 70 69 68 67 66 65 64 63 62 61 60 59 58 57 56 55 234
73 74 75 76 77 78 79 80 81 82 83 84 85 86 87 88 89 90 235
82 S 83 S 84 S 85 S 86 S 87 S 88 S 89 S 90 S

Column 3

Soldier's Monument

1	2	3	4	5	6	7	8	9	10	210
20	19	18	17	16	15	14	13	12	11	211
21	22 ■	23	24 ▲	25 ◆	26	27	28	29 ■	30	230
40	39	38	37	36	35 ■	34	33	32	31	231
41	42	43 ●	44	45	46	47	48	49	50	250
241	242	243	244	245 ■	246	247 ▲	248	249	251	252

A	B	C	D	201	A	B	C	D	205	A	B	C	D	219
E	F ■	G	H	202	E	F ■	G ●	H	206	E	F	G	H	220
209	210	211	212	213	214	215	216	217	218	219	220	221	222	221
A	B	C	D ■▲	203	A	B	C ■	D	207	A	B	C	D	240
E	F	G	H	204	E	F	G	H	208	E	F	G	H	241

A	B	C	D	201	A	B	C	D	205	A	B	C ◆	D	201
E	F	G	H	202	E	F	G	H	206	E ●	F ●	G	H ■	204
209	210	211	212	213	214	215	216	217	218	219	220	221	222	205
A	B	C	D	203	A	B	C	D	207	A	B	C	D ◆■	208
E	F	G	H	204	E	F	G	H	208	E	F	G	H	209

A	A 3 B	A 2 B	1	1	2	3	4	5 ■

6	5	4	3	2	1	40	39	38	37	238
206	205	204	203	202	201	244	245	246	247	239
7	8	9	10	11	12	33	34	35	36	240
207	208	209	210	211	212	233	234	235	236	241
18	17	16	15	14	13	32	31	30	29	242
218	217	216	215	214	213	212	231	230	229	243 ▲
19	20	21	22	23	24	25	26	27	28	228
206	205	204	203 ♦	202	201	240	239	238	237	241
6	5	4	3	2	1	40	39	38	37	242
227	228	209	210	211	212	233	240	239	215	243
7	8	9	10	11	12	33	34	35	36	244
216	217	216	215	214	213	212	211	230	229	245
18	17	16	15	14	13	32	31	30	29	246
216	220	221	222	223	224	225	226	227	228	247
19	20	21	22 ♦	23	24	25	26	27	28	248
201	202	203 ▲♦	204	205	206	207 ♦	208	209 ▲	210	212
1	2	3 ▲	4	5	6 ■	7	8	9	10	213
20	19 ♦	18	17	16 ■	15	14	13	12	11	211 ♦
21	22	23	24	25	26	27	28 ●	29	30	230 ▲
40	39	38	37	36	35	34	33	32	31	231
41	42	43	44	45	46	47	48	49 ■	50 ♦	252

1	2 ♦	3	4	5 *	6	7	8	9	10	210
20	19	18 ●	17	16	15	14	13	12	11	211
21	22	23 *	24	25	26 ▲	27	28	29	30	230
40	39	38	37	36	35	34	33	32	31	231
41	42	43	44	45 ●	46	47	48	49	50	250
201	202	203	204	205 ♦	206	207	208	209 ♦	210	211
1 ♦	2	3	4	5	6	7	8	9	10	212
20	19	18	17	16	15 *	14	13	12	11	211
21	22	23 ▲■	24	25	26	27	28	29	30 ■	230
40	39 ■	38	37	36	35	34	33	32	31	231
41	42	43	44	45	46	47	48	49	50	250

1	2	3	4	5	6	7	8	9	10 ♦	211
20	19 ♦	18	17	16	15	14	13	12	11	212
21	22	23	24	25	26	27	28	29	30	230
40	39	38	37	36	35	34	33	32	31 ♦	231
41	42	43	44	45	46	47 ●	48	49	50	250
41/5	42/5	43/5	44/5	45/5	46/5	47/5	48/5	49/5	50/5	250/5

Column 5

| 6 | 7 | 8 ▲ | 9 | 10 | 11 | 12 | 13 | 14 | 15 |

1	2	3	4	5	6	7	8	9	10
20	19	18 ●	17	16	15	14	13 ■	12	11
21	22	23	24	25	26	27	28	29	30
40	39	38	37	36	35	34	33	32	31
41	42	43	44	45	46	47	48	49	50
60	59	58	57	56	55	54	53	52	51
61	62	63	64	65	66	67	68 ●	69	70
80 ▲	79	78	77	76	75	74	73	72 ■	71
81	82	83	84	85	86 ■	87	88	89	90
100	99	98	97	96	95	94	93	92	91
201	202 ■	203	204	205	206	207	208	209	210
1	2	3	4	5	6	7	8	9	10
20	19	18	17	16	15	14	13	12 *	11
21	22	23	24	25	26	27	28	29	30 ■
40 ■	39	38	37	38	35	34	33	32	31
41	42	43	44	45	46	47	48	49	50 ●

1	2	3 ●	4	5	6 ■	7	8	9	10
20	19	18	17	16	15	14	13	12	11
21	22	23	24	25	26	27	28	29	30
40	39	38	37	36	35	34	33	32	31
41	42	43	44	45	46	47	48	49	50
201	202	203	204	205	206	207 ●	208	209 ●	210
1	2	3 ■	4	5	6	7	8	9	10
20	19	18	17	16	15	14	13	12	11
31	22	23	24	25	26	27	28	29	30
40 ✻	39	38 ●	37	36	35	34 ◆	33	32	31
41 ●	42	43	44	45	46	47	48	49	50

1	2	3	4	5	6	7 ●	8	9	10
20 ✻	19	18	17	16	15	14	13	12	11
21	22	23	24	25	26	27	28	29	30
40	39	38	37	36	35	34	33	32	31
41 ●	42	43	44	45 ●	46	47	48	49	50
41/5	42/5	43/5	44/5	45/5	46/5	46/5 ●	48/5	49/5	50/5

A	B	1	2	3	4	5	6	7	8	9	10	11	12
		●				●		* ●				●	

	1	2	3	4	5	6	7	8	9	10	11	12
201	1 *	2	3	4	5 ■	6	7 ●	8	9	10	11	12 ●
224	24 ●	23	22	21	20	19	18	17	16 *	15	14	13
225	25	26	27	28	29	30	31	32	33	34	35	36
248	48	47	46	45	44	43	42	41 ◆	40	39	38	37
249	49	50	51	52	53	54	55	56	57	58	59	60
272	72	71	70 ●	69	68 ●	67	66	65	64	63	62	61 ●
273 ■	73	74	75	76	77	78	79 *	80	81	82	83	84
256	96	95	94	93	92	91	90	89	88	87	86	85
257	97	98 ●	99	100	101	102	103	104	105	106 ●	107	108 ●
220 ●	120	119	118	117	116	115	114	113	112	111	110	109
221	121	122	123	124	125	126	127	128	129	130	131	132
249	144	143	142	141	140	139	138	137	136	135	134	133
222	201	202	203	204	205	206	207	208	209	210	211	212
223	1	2	3	4	5	6	7	8 *	9	10	11	12
224	24	23	22	21 ◆	20	19	18	17	16	15	14	13
225	25	26 *	27	28	29	30	31	32	33	34	35	36
248	48	47	46	45	44	43	42	41	40	39	38	37
249	49	50	51	52	53 ◆	54	55	56	57	58	59	60
272	72	71	70 ●	69	68	67	66	65	64	63	62	61

201	1	2	3	4	5	6	7	8	9	10	11	12
224	24	23	22	21	20	19	18	17	16	15	14	13
225	25	26	27	28	29	30	11	32	33	34	35	36
248	48	47	46	45	44	43	42	41	40	39	38	37
249	49	50	51	52	53	54	55	56	57	58	59	60
272	72	71	70	69	68	67	66	65	64	63	62	61
222	201	202	203	204	205	206	207	208	209	210	211	212
223	1	2	3	4	5	6	7	8	9	10	11	12
224	24	23	22	21	20	19	18	17	16	15	14	13
225	25	26	27	28	29	30	31	32	33	34	35	36
248	48	47	46	45	44	43	42	41	40	39	38	37
249	49	50	51	52	53	54	55	56	57	58	59	60
272	72	71	70	69	68	67	66	65	64	63	62	61

201	1	2	3	4	5	6	7	8	9	10	11	12
224	24	23	22	21	20	19	18	17	16	15	14	13
225	25	26	27	28	29	30	31	32	33	34	35	36
248	48	47	46	45	44	43	42	41	40	39	38	37
249	49	50	51	52	53	54	55	56	57	58	59	60
272	72	71	70	69	68	67	66	65	64	63	62	61
272/5	72/5	71/5	70/5	69/5	68/5	67/5	66/5	65/5	64/5	63/5	62/5	61/5

Column 7

| 1 | 2 | 3 | 4 | 5 | 6 | 7 | 8 | 9 | 10 | 11 | 12 | 13 | 14 | 15 | 16 | 17 | 18 |

1	2	3	4	5	6	7	8	9	10	11	12	13	14	15	16	216	217
32	31	30	29	28	27	26	25	24	23	22	21	20	19	18	17	219	218
33	34	35	36	37	38	39	40	41	42	43	44	45	46	47	48	220	221
64	63	62	61	60	59	58	57	56	55	54	53	52	51	50	49	223	222
65	66	67	68	69	70	71	72	73	74	75	76	77	78	79	80	224	225
96	95	94	93	92	91	90	89	88	87	86	85	84	83	82	81	227	226
97	98	99	100	101	102	103	104	105	106	107	108	109	110	111	112	228	229
128	127	126	125	124	123	122	121	120	119	118	117	116	115	114	113	231	230
129	130	131	132	133	134	135	136	137	138	139	140	141	142	143	144	232	233
160	159	158	157	156	155	154	153	152	151	150	149	148	147	146	145	235	234
161	162	163	164	165	166	167	168	169	170	171	172	173	174	175	176	236	237
192	191	190	189	188	187	186	185	184	183	182	181	180	179	178	177	239	238
201	202	203	204	205	206	207	208	209	210	211	212	213	214	215	216	217	218
1	2	3	4	5	6	7	8	9	10	11	12	13	14	15	16	220	219
32	31	30	29	28	27	26	25	24	23	22	21	20	19	18	17	221	222
33	34	35	36	37	38	39	40	41	42	43	44	45	46	47	48	224	223
64	63	62	61	60	59	58	57	56	55	54	53	52	51	50	49	225	226
65	66	67	68	69	70	71	72	73	74	75	76	77	78	79	80	228	227
96		94	93	92	91	90	89	88	87	86	85	84	83	82	81	229	230

1	2	3	4	5	6	7	8	9	10	11	12	13	14	15	16	217	218
32	31	30	29	28	27	26	25	24	23	22	21	20	19	18	17	220	219
33	34	35	36	37	38	39	40	41	42	43	44	45	46	47	48	221	222
64	63	62	61	60	59	58	57	56	55	54	53	52	51	50	49	224	223
65	66	67	68	69	70	71	72	73	74	75	76	77	78	79	80	225	226
96	95	94	93	92	91	90	89	88	87	86	85	84	83	82	81	228	227
201	202	203	204	205	206	207	208	209	210	211	212	213	214	215	216	217	218

1	2	3	4	5	6	7	8	9	10	11	12	13	14	15	16	220	219
32	31	30	29	28	27	26	25	24	23	22	21	20	19	18	17	221	222
33	34	35	36	37	38	39	40	41	42	43	44	45	46	47	48	224	223
64	63	62	61	60	59	58	57	56	55	54	53	52	51	50	49	225	226
65	66	67	68	69	70	71	72	73	74	75	76	77	78	79	80	228	227
96	95	94	93	92	91	90	89	88	87	86	85	84	83	82	81	229	230
295	295	294	293	292	291	290	289	288	287	286	285	284	283	282	281	232	231

1	2	3	4	5	6	7	8	9	10	11	12	13	14	15	16	17	18	118
36	35	34	33	32	31	30	29	28	27	26	25	24	23	22	21	20	19	119
37	38	39	40	41	42	43	44	45	46	47	48	49	50	51	52	53	54	120
72	71	70	69	68	67	66	65	64	63	62	61	60	59	58	57	56	55	155
73	74	75	76	77	78	79	80	81	82	83	84	85	86	87	88	89	90	190
108	107	106	105	104	103	102	101	100	99	98	97	96	95	94	93	92	91	191

Made in the USA
Coppell, TX
14 October 2021